Radical
CLASSICISM

The Architecture of
QUINLAN TERRY

Forecourt

Cars

Kitchen

B'fast

Entrance

Study

Shed

Lobby

Hall

Dining

Drawing Room

Loggia

Ground Floor Plan

Entrance

Radical
CLASSICISM

The Architecture of
QUINLAN TERRY

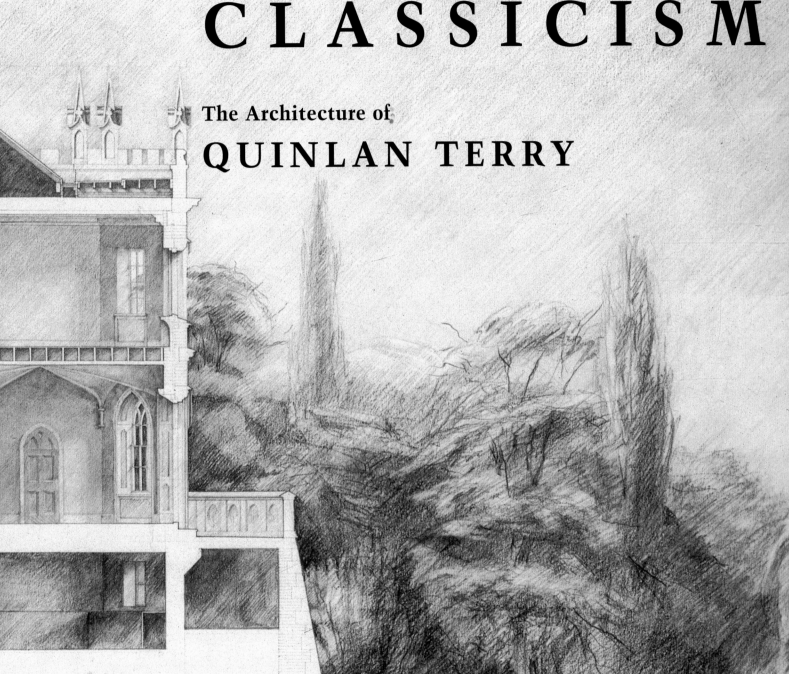

David Watkin

RIZZOLI
NEW YORK

First published in the United States of America in 2006 by
RIZZOLI INTERNATIONAL PUBLICATIONS, INC.
300 Park Avenue South, New York, NY 10010
www.rizzoliusa.com

ISBN-10: 0-8478-2806-9
ISBN-13: 9-780847-828067
LCCN: 2005933926

Photography Credits: Please see page 256.

Designed by Abigail Sturges

Printed and bound in China

2006 2007 2008 2009 2010 / 10 9 8 7 6 5 4 3 2 1

Contents

I have followed Quinlan Terry's career for many years, and taken great interest in what has been a remarkable, challenging and, I hope, rewarding life spent studying and practising great architecture. Remarkable, because through a period where the classical tradition has been consistently derided or ignored, he has followed his calling to keep alive and practise the sensible, intellectually rigorous and grammatical discipline of classicism. I am sure that many others share my admiration for the way he has not only made the classical tradition his lifetime's study, but that his practice has afforded opportunities to test and develop history's precedents in the present day.

Challenging, because his whole career has been spent in direct opposition to the architectural mainstream, whose theory – Modernism - necessitates the ruthless negation of the past. This has meant that despite his achievements refining the essentially reasonable and practical aspects of Classical architecture his professional path must have been often a lonely one.

Rewarding, because through his commitment to this difficult course he has been able to enjoy the functional, durable, dependable, orderly and expressive nature of classical architecture. I know through personal contact and his writings that Quin has a sincere concern for the nature of beauty which means he values not only proportion and fitness for purpose, but also decoration and rich display. In this, his work truly satisfies the third of Vitruvius's maxims for architectural design: *delight*.

A note should perhaps be made of some of the practical achievements documented in this book. He builds sympathetically in sensitive historic environments, evidenced at Merchants' Square in Colonial Williamsburg and, of course, at our own Richmond Riverside in England where enhanced value has been obtained by his clients over the long term. He uses traditional materials adeptly – often locally sourced – with the confidence that they will last for centuries. Mention must also be made of the appropriateness with which he approaches each commission; his attention to the context, scale and use of the building in question, a world away from the "house style" of so many current practitioners. His work, wherever it shows a public face, has an indisputably restorative effect on the urban setting, often succeeding to repair damaging interruptions to streetscapes and important vistas. Meanwhile, his use of ornament and decoration provides wonderful opportunities for the deployment of an all-too-threatened breed of skilled craftsmen.

Finally, Quinlan Terry's architecture, employing as it does natural materials in a manner derived from place-based tradition, has made a great contribution in defining a more sustainable approach to architecture – one that recognizes the ecological qualities inherent in traditional building, and incorporates contemporary environmental lessons in a contextual manner. It is interesting to see a number of his earlier works, built in the 1960's and 1970's, illustrated in this book. They show that when proper traditional detailing and materials are used the buildings not only last (surely a prime consideration as regards "sustainability?"), but tend to improve in appearance with time. True sustainability is intergenerational, and I do not doubt that Quinlan Terry's buildings will be performing well and delighting their users long after much of the high-tech 'ecotecture' and Deconstructivist signature building of the present day has worn out.

One of the great joys of this book is the number of pen and ink drawings from the sketchbooks of both Quin and his remarkably talented son, Francis. Sadly, fewer and fewer architects today seem to enjoy sketching, partly, no doubt, because they think the past has little to teach them. Personally, I would not employ an architect who could not draw well or express his or her ideas through the medium of pen and ink or pencil. Such a facility was of enormous importance to the Foundation Course at my former Institute of Architecture and, indeed, my current Drawing School has grown out of the life classes that were an essential feature of this Course. An ability to draw well does not preclude the use of computer-aided design techniques – far from it. It merely ensures that man remains the master of new technology, used appropriately, as a genuine aid, rather than the slave.

Thus it is easy for me to find delight in Quinlan Terry's work and I hope the same will be true for the readers of this book. In every way he exemplifies tradition as defined by Goethe: "tending the fire, not the ashes". And he more than fulfils Goethe's dictum that "architecture is frozen music".

Quinlan and Francis Terry at work, Old Exchange, Dedham, Essex, 2004

Introduction

Quinlan Terry is the single most distinguished and prolific architect at work in the classical tradition in either Britain or the United States of America. He has attempted more completely than any other architect in Britain to pull the rug from beneath the false certainties of Modernism. At the same time, he is both modern and radical for, as he rightly claims, "no one has the monopoly of the word 'Modern'"; but why should we also call him radical? The answer is that Modernism, itself once a radical movement, is now a stale and tired orthodoxy that denies the human demand for poetry, beauty, order, harmony, tradition, and reason. To overthrow it and reinstate classical architecture as eternally new, beautiful, stable, and sane, has been about the most radical and challenging ambition any architect in the second half of the twentieth century could have had. Terry's life and career have had to be a continuous and sometimes almost solitary battle against the architectural establishment and even, on occasion, the conservation world. He believes that the campaign against the Modernist orthodoxy that he and his fellow classical and traditional architects have been forced to conduct is a unique chapter in the history of architecture, presenting them with difficulties that no previous generation of classical architects has had to face. However, the numerous beautiful plates in this book are a testimony both to his undeviating adherence to his principles, and also to his increasingly numerous patrons, public and private, who have rejected the beliefs of the current architectural profession in favor of the values of our forefathers.

Indeed, a more benign climate is finally emerging in England and in the U.S.A., where he was awarded the Richard H. Driehaus Prize for Classical Architecture in 2005. This annual award of $100,000 was established in 2003 in deliberate rivalry to the Modernist Pritzker Prize, the first two winners being Léon Krier and Demetri Porphyrios. Terry has also been invited to provide new buildings in London in Baker Street and in Tottenham Court Road to replace Modernist proposals that were found unsuitable to their settings by planning officers. He has been extensively employed in America in both residential and commercial buildings such as Highland Park House, Dallas, and Merchants Square, Colonial Williamsburg. Even more unusually, by building in Berlin, Frankfurt, and Munich, he has been able to return German architecture to its classical roots. This is a remarkable achievement because there is no country in Europe in which, on spurious moral grounds, it has been more difficult to use the classical language since World War II.

Classicism is a language with a grammar, so that its use by ill-informed architects since the World War II on both sides of the Atlantic has made it an easy prey for ridicule from the Modernists. Nonetheless, Modernism has been unsuccessful in providing popular images of domesticity, so that the dull or ignorant neo-Georgianism which the Modernists criticize is often produced for the housing market in response to the call by the public for traditional homes. One of the differences between the radical classicism of Quinlan Terry and third-rate uninspired classicism is the infinite care he gives to every detail of the classical language of which he has acquired enormous knowledge. Radical, too, is his stress on the vital importance of ornament, condemned as "crime" by Modernism but shining through in every plate in this book. He has also been radical in showing in Richmond and London that historic town centers can take large, modern commercial buildings without being overwhelmed or wrecked. His Brentwood Cathedral is a radical statement as virtually the only major Roman Catholic church following the Second Vatican Council that is in harmony with the traditional forms of classical architecture and at the same time strikingly novel. He can shock and entertain, as in his curvaceous Corinthian Villa in Regent's Park or Fawley House, Oxfordshire, which produce an electric effect with their startling movement.

At every point in his still-developing career, the work of Quinlan Terry has been shot through with a profound sense of place and of history. His buildings have that appropriateness to local setting, to historical environment, and to traditional materials, which the totalitarian arrogance of Modernism has aimed to destroy. He demonstrates a feeling for public decorum that finds its natural expression in what in the eighteenth century, following the ancient world, was called civic virtue. This explains his work at Richmond Riverside, Baker Street, and Colonial Williamsburg, where, respecting the environment, he roots his interventions in an outward modesty before the past, combined with an inner joy at the privilege he feels in belonging to the classical tradition which links us with the fathers of our civilization.

Raymond Erith at Bridges Farm, Dedham, Essex, 1959

The Role of Raymond Erith

Quinlan Terry is pleased to acknowledge his debt as an architect and draftsman to Raymond Erith (1904–1973), of whom he was a pupil from 1962 and a partner from 1966. An architect of exceptional skill and sensitivity, Erith followed a lonely path in his devotion to traditional values in architecture, notably during the 1950s and 60s, the nadir of architecture and planning in Britain. Despite the hostility of the professional architectural establishment to Erith's designs, his abilities won him important commissions from many discerning patrons, notably at Lady Margaret Hall, Oxford, Jack Straw's Castle, Hampstead Heath, the New Common Room Building at Gray's Inn, and numerous houses and cottages in the country. He also carried out major reconstruction work and substantial new building at nos. 10–12, Downing Street, where his anti-Modernist and anti-Zeitgeist philosophy is perfectly expressed in his statement, "I do not intend to leave my mark on the additions in Downing Street, nor on no. 12. I attach no importance at all to originality or modernity and I shall be content to carry on in a way which is not very different from the other buildings." Ironically, despite this engaging modesty, his additions were so far-reaching that English Heritage regulations would today condemn them for "falsifying history" by adding new, traditionally designed elements to historic buildings. Something "frankly modern," true to the "spirit of the age," would now be recommended, probably a glass infill which, as leading Modernists are fond of claiming about a variety of new buildings, would represent "the openness of democracy."

Terry's love of Baroque, notably of Borromini, led to fruitful debate between him and Erith, who was less enamored of the style. "I am a Puritan." he would say to Terry, "you are a Jesuit, and there, but for the grace of me, go you!" Yet Terry designed a handsome Baroque organ case in memory of Erith in 1976 in the Georgian church of St Mary, Paddington Green, which he and Erith had restored in 1972–73. The belief in continuity inherent in the classical tradition leads Terry to feel that he stands in an interesting position between his master, Raymond Erith, and his son, Francis Terry, born in 1969. He notes that the practice has continued for nearly eighty years, with fresh input from himself and his son. It was called Erith and Terry from 1966, but the name was changed to Quinlan and Francis Terry in 2003, thirty years after Erith's death. Terry likes to contemplate the value to Robert Adam of being the son of William Adam, a practicing architect, and of similar relations in the Wyatt, Cockerell, and Scott families of architects. Remarkably, thirty-seven members of the Wyatt family were engaged in architecture and the allied trades throughout the eighteenth and nineteenth centuries. Such dynasties were more common in seventeenth- and eighteenth-century France, where families such as the Mansarts and the Gabriels were concerned to promote an inherited public language.

The Personality of a Practice

Quinlan Terry's career began slowly with minor country buildings from the 1960s to the late 1970s, but a turning point was Raymond Erith's last commission for a country house, King's Walden Bury, Hertfordshire, for Sir Thomas Pilkington, Bart., in 1968. At the time when it was built in 1968–71, it was widely supposed that it would be the last new country house ever built in Britain, for it is impossible to exaggerate the extent to which in 1968 it was held that there was no alternative to Modernism for a large building, or indeed for any building. Evidence about the survival of traditional and classical architecture was, and indeed, still is, ignored in architectural journals, rather as free thought was in Soviet Russia.

The situation was different in America where the ideology of Modernism had achieved a totalitarian stranglehold only in large urban developments. Rich men were always able to commission private buildings in the countryside in traditional styles. In England, after 1945, the stranglehold was double-edged in that it condemned both traditional styles in architecture, and also traditional wealth. Taxation, which remained at 98 percent on investment income until the 1980s, prevented people from erecting ambitious private buildings in the classical, or any style. However, Terry has since then produced a remarkable chain of country houses in England and the U.S.A., each with a special relation to the needs and character of the client and the setting. Sensitivity to historical environment informed, as we shall see, Terry's Richmond Riverside, new buildings at Downing College, Cambridge, and his internal additions at no. 10, Downing Street.

Terry also understands the human joy in ornament that Modernism has outlawed. His work thus demonstrates the fruits of his realization that Renaissance architects adorned the surface of their buildings with ornamental forms that were scarcely sanctioned by antiquity, such as brackets, balustrades, parapets, masks, and frames. The writings of Vitruvius and Alberti are more or less silent on topics like the placement of astragals, of egg and dart mouldings, and of sculpture, while even Palladio avoids discussion of sculpture, despite the

prominence of it in his own buildings. Terry has thus faced a difficult task in reconstructing this practice. Modernist architects neither wish to design moldings and ornaments, nor are capable of doing so. However, they should remember that Sir John Soane, who always referred to architects as "artists," told his pupils that,

> The art of profiling and enriching the different assemblages of moldings, although now much neglected, is of the highest importance to the perfection of architecture. Perhaps the mind of a great artist is never more visible to the judicious observer than in this part of his profession, for profiles and assemblages of moldings are in architecture similar and of equal importance with those indescribable elegancies in poetry and painting which are not always sufficiently felt nor fully appreciated.

To master the complex language of moldings that Terry has undertaken requires a lifetime of learning, observation, and drawing. With a functional origin in casting off rain, they have a curvaceous beauty of their own that imparts great variety and life to a building by the changing shadows that they cast as the sunlight moves around during the day, as can be appreciated in many photographs of moldings in this book. Their design involves knowledge of sciagraphy, the branch of the science of perspective dealing with the production of shadows, derived from *skia*, the Greek word for shadow. Here is Terry's explanation of the role of drawing in his practice:

12

I prepare my drawings freehand in the traditional manner without the assistance of computer-drawing facilities. One of the advantages of drawing and redrawing freehand is that it forces me to reconsider the overall composition of the design as the project develops. This is a process both interesting and enjoyable; it is fundamental to my work as I progress from 1:200 scale drawings to 1:50 scale and later to 1:10 scale and full size, during which time minor detailed variations are incorporated. This approach is, of course, similar to that of all the classical architects of the past.

It is also a striking aspect of the Terrys' office that a house drawing style has been established within it, so that a common hand can be discerned in drawings by Francis Terry and the other young architects working with him.

The Religion of Modernism

The Modernism, with which Quinlan Terry has had to battle, is like the Taliban, a puritanical religion, so iconoclastic that it permits no reference whatever to the forms, materials, or methods of construction of traditional, classical, or vernacular language, and above all no use of moldings. It demands such total commitment that no one can opt out of it without fear of being labeled a cultural, intellectual, and social outcast. It has acquired control over education so that the practice of traditional and classical architecture is not taught as a major program in any school of architecture in Britain, and in only one in the U.S.A. Modernism needs to present a permanent face of revolution in order to maintain its overall control. To be successful as the sole victor, it requires a constant enemy, and the most permanent enemy is the past.

Modernism everywhere requires the worship of the new. Advanced Modernist buildings being put up today by leading architects are well known for their frequent structural weaknesses and impractibility, involving experimental construction techniques and materials, and vast areas of glass. These monuments to vanity by architectural prima donnas are "signature buildings," yet often require remodeling and adaptation within a few years, sometimes months, of completion. Genuine classical buildings improve with age because of their use of traditional materials and detailing, unlike Modernist buildings, which look glamorous and shiny, especially in photographs, on completion, but slowly deteriorate. Where the Modernists build for a few decades, Terry builds for hundreds of years, as our forefathers did: indeed, the Crown Estate recently extended the lease on his buildings in Regent's Park to 150 years, assuming without question that they would last that long! One wonders what the life of buildings by leading Modernists will be. To see how Terry's work has already improved with the passing of time, one has only to turn to the photographs in this book of buildings like his Bibury Court and its summer house, Pin Oak, Kentucky, and the Howard Building at Downing College.

Terry's devotion to the many craftsmen who make his buildings possible reminds him of a verse from Rudyard Kipling:

Who lest all thought of Eden fade,
Bring'st Eden to the craftsman's brain
Godlike to muse o'er his own trade
And Manlike to stand with God again.

The present book thus contains photographs of some of these skilled stonemasons, plasterers, and joiners, at work. Terry believes that modern building practice, controlled by each new edition of the Building Regulations, is relentlessly creating an unwholesome environment. To save heat, buildings are now hermetically sealed with double glazing and with seals around the opening parts, like a motor car. If air conditioning is to function economically, virtually all the air has to be recycled, causing SBS (sick building syndrome), Black Mould, and the spread of respiratory failures such as Legionnaire's disease. Previous generations understood that humans, like the animal kingdom, need plenty of ventilation. The materials they used, stone, brickwork in lime not cement mortar, timber, and slate, are not only visually appealing but largely inert to changes in temperature. Thus they do not require frequent expansion joints as do concrete, steel, bricks in cement mortar, aluminium, and plastics. If modern buildings have a short life span of less than fifty years, their capital costs have to be repeated, which is not only financial insanity, but also does very real damage to the environment because modern materials cannot be recycled. Indeed, eventually there will be no licensed tips in which to receive the damaging products used in their construction. Sir Christopher Wren, by contrast, wrote that "Architecture aims at eternity," whereas a Modernist building does not even make an attractive ruin.

One of the reasons for the description of Terry as "radical" in this book is precisely his rejection of the values and practices of the entire architectural establishment. In "My Kind of Town," a paper he published in *Architecture Today* in 2005, he explained his admiration for the city of Rome, asking,

> How is it that these buildings endure for centuries—even millennia and don't have to be constantly demolished and rebuilt after a few decades? How is it that people have lived in these buildings for so long without the modern requirements of lifts, air-conditioning, heating, and electricity? How is it that the rooms are naturally cool in summer and warm in winter? The answer is simple. They built thick walls in brick, lime mortar, and stone; their floors and roofs were constructed in timber and covered in clay tiles. They could not build higher than six stories, and had to consider the size and position of windows in relation to the rooms behind them because that would determine their comfort and survival. They did not have the option of using reinforced concrete, modern cement, large sheets of glass, and plastics; and they did not have the luxury of burning up the resources of the earth – oil, coal, and gas. Thus they had a sustainable environment and a sustainable future which we in our extravagant and now precarious world can no longer sustain because of the dogma of Modernism.

Sustainability and longevity are among the keynotes of Terry's work, which is thus in marked contrast to the glass and steel buildings of modern prima donna architects, high in energy consumption.

In addition, Terry, like other current traditional architects such as Demetri Porphyrios, realizes that imitation, the Greek mimesis, has been a constant feature of architecture from the earliest times. Properly done, it is a difficult process, not an easy one. For example, in his published essay, "Seven Misunderstandings about Classical Architecture," Terry points out that if you want to design a door in the Palladian manner, you discover that in his *I Quattro Libri* Palladio gives only "the proportions and profile of the moldings. No guidance is given on size, scale, materials, or methods of construction." Thus, though Palladio is the most imitated architect in history, anyone who attempts to follow him has to return to roots and start from scratch. As Lutyens famously wrote,

That time-worn doric order—a lovely thing—I have the cheek to adopt. You can't copy it. To be right, you have to take it and design it . . . . It means hard labor, hard thinking over every line in all three dimensions and in every joint . . . . If you tackle it in this way, the Order belongs to you, and every stroke, being mentally handled, must become endowed with such power and artistry as God has given you.

Tradition is Controversy

Quinlan Terry is seen as a radical by both the Modernist architectural establishment and by sections of the conservation world. He finds that planning legislation involves interference by people with no knowledge of building construction and sometimes indoctrinated with a blinkered Modernism. An early controversy was the rejection of the residential development that he and Raymond Erith designed in 1966–67 at Shottesbrooke, Berkshire, for Sir John Smith, founder of the Landmark Trust. Their proposal was for a closed quadrangle of twelve single-story houses for the elderly, designed in a partly Georgian and partly castellated style. Aligned on an avenue of lime trees in axis with the tower of the medieval parish church, they were to be built on land given by Sir John Smith to the local authority. However, the scheme was rejected by the county planning authority, partly because in the brave new world of "modern man," it was thought distressing for the old to look at a church and a grave yard.

More recent work has been considered so controversial that it has led to planning appeals, notably at Brentwood Cathedral, St Helen's, Bishopsgate, Baker Street, and Great Canfield. However, these have created precedents, for example at Baker Street, which led to changes in the City of Westminster planning guides in conservation areas, recommending load-bearing masonry construction, traditional materials, and sash windows; while Great Canfield was the first country house to be built under the new PPG7 planning exemption which allowed local authorities to grant permission for buildings on agricultural land, which are considered outstanding in architectural and landscape terms. Terry's designs for a new infirmary next to Sir Christopher Wren's Royal Hospital Chelsea (1682–92) received planning consent in 2005 from all the relevant authorities: English Heritage, CABE (Commission for Architecture and the Built Environment), and the Royal Borough of Kensington and Chelsea. Astonishingly, the leading Modernist architect, Lord Rogers, intervened by asking the Secretary of State to have Terry's plans called in for a public inquiry. Such is the intensity of the opposition of the architectural establishment to Terry's buildings.

By contrast, his major urban works, from Richmond Riverside in 1984–87 to Baker Street in 2002, have brought great joy to the general public, even if they have been criticized by leading Modernists as "false" facades to commercial office interiors. This is because in the needless pursuit of the doctrine of "truth" in the religion of Modernist architecture, it has been insisted that interior and exterior should always be one and the same thing. However, the complex story of architecture teaches us a very different lesson: Alberti at the Palazzo Rucellai and at several churches, Palladio at the Basilica at Vicenza, and Jones at Old St Paul's, all produced exteriors that bear no relation to their interiors. By contrast, Adam at Syon House and Soane at the Law Courts produced interiors that bear no relation to their exteriors. Also, Modernists do not practice what they preach: their buildings are invariably faced with a veneer of glass, brick, or even stone, concealing a steel or concrete frame. In tra-

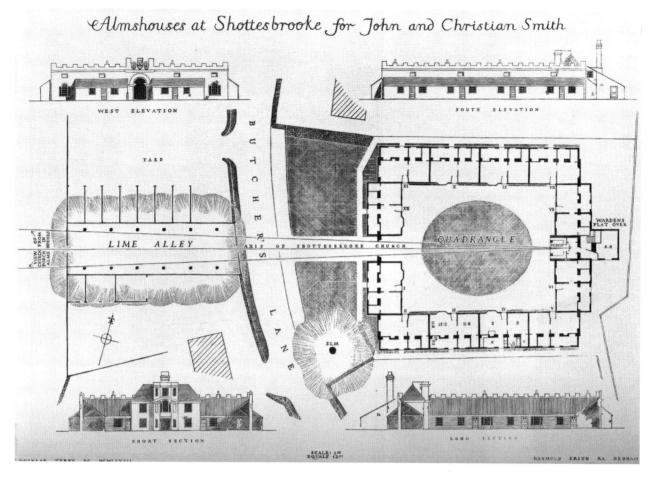

Almshouses at Shottesbrooke for John and Christian Smith

WEST ELEVATION

SOUTH ELEVATION

YARD

BUTCHER'S LANE

LIME ALLEY

AXIS OF SHOTTESBROOKE CHURCH

QUADRANGLE

WARDENS FLAT OVER

VIEW OF CHURCH FROM PORCH OF ALMS HOUSES

PORCH

ELM

SHORT SECTION

LONG SECTION

SCALE: 1 IN
EQUALS 12 FT

RAYMOND ERITH RA DEDHAM

*Raymond Erith and
Quinlan Terry, design
for almshouses,
Shottesbrooke,
Berkshire, 1968.
Linocut by Quinlan
Terry, exhibited at
the Royal Academy
Summer Exhibition,
1968*

ditional buildings, by contrast, the masonry walls that you see on the outside support the floors and roof. Which of these types of building, traditionalist or Modernist, should thus be branded as merely facadist?

Urbanism may be seen as constituting a special case within this category, for what is of prime importance is the creation of street and square to provide an appealing urban scenery. Interiors, especially in commercial buildings, are of lesser significance as they are likely to be ephemeral. John Nash understood this in his terraces in Regent's Park and also in Carlton House Terrace (1827–33), where he was content for other architects to design interiors and even rear elevations. He was following in the tradition by which in 1698 the city of Paris recognized the importance of building the imposing facades of the Place Vendôme, designed by Jules Hardouin-Mansart, so that the new square would have a unified, permanent, and dignified character. The city then sold the lots behind the facades to individual owners, mainly financiers, who could employ their own architects and designers to provide them with what was currently fashionable in terms of disposition and decoration.

Art or Theory

The rise of the history of art and architecture as an academic subject undertaken by scholars and theorists, and not, as in the past, by artists or architects, has meant that some art historians, unfamiliar with the process of patronage at a high level, do not appreciate the extent to which the architect, even one of strong opinions and great knowledge like Quinlan Terry, may have to accommodate himself to his patron's wishes. Inheriting from the nineteenth century a romantic image of the artist as a solitary romantic genius, art historians may thus misinterpret modern works, as well as those of the Renaissance and Baroque periods, by failing to understand the input of the patron.

The Renaissance was fueled by study of Vitruvius, whose *Ten Books of Architecture*, written in circa 25 BC, consisted largely of practical advice, not theory. The same was true of Palladio's *I Quattro Libri dell'Architettura* (1570), a work almost as influential as Vitruvius, while Geoffrey Scott wisely observed in his masterly book, *The Architecture of Humanism* (1914), that "the attempt to decide architectural right and wrong purely on intellectual grounds is precisely one of the roots of our mischief. Theory, I suppose, was what made the chatter on the scaffolding on the Tower of Babel." As Quinlan Terry himself observed in *Architects Anonymous* (1984):

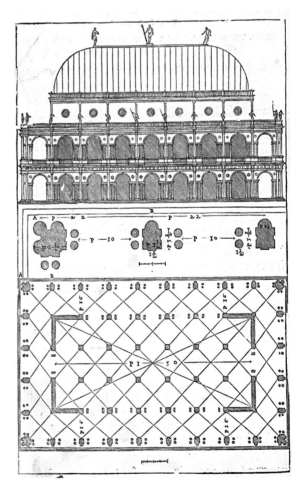

Basilica, Vicenza (1549–80), from Palladio, I Quattro Libri *(1570)*

> When a twentieth-century Vanbrugh or Gibbs—or even a latter-day Nash—is commissioned to work on any old building, he is restricted from designing in the old tradition on the grounds that this would falsify history. The historical continuity of classicism was approved throughout the seventeenth, eighteenth, and nineteenth centuries but is forbidden in the twentieth. What is called "genuine" in all the revivals up to the turn of this century is called "pastiche" in this. Thus the continuity of architectural history is paralyzed, ironically, by the nostrums of architectural historians; and the rise of architectural history as an academic degree subject runs parallel with the demise of classical architecture. Architecture has become something to be written about—not to be looked at, or built today—the written word counts for more than the visual image.

Indeed, for thousands of years architects spoke through their buildings and it was not until architecture acquired the trappings of a religion that it required a justificatory gospel. It is evidence of the inadequacy of contemporary architecture that it is forced to prop itself up in laborious, pretentious, and often unreadable verbiage. It is hoped that the photographs of architecture and its ornamental details in this book will be found so stunningly beautiful in their own right that no such rhetoric is required to justify them.

CHAPTER 1

Urban and Commercial Buildings

Gray's Inn

London

Like the elder and younger Wood in Bath, John Nash (1752–1835) in Regent Street, and C. R. Cockerell (1788–1863) in the city of London, Quinlan Terry brings the virtues of dignified Classicism to property development and commercial buildings. This central aspect of his career began with his work on the drawings for Raymond Erith's Common Room Building at Gray's Inn in London (1970–72). Eleven bays long and four stories high with a central pediment, this is in effect an office building, despite its historic setting within the heart of one of London's four Inns of Court. With its Baroque doorcase and Georgian Gothick wing linking it to the Hall, it introduced Terry to the concept of instant history in new buildings.

PREVIOUS PAGES
*Richmond Riverside,
Richmond-on-
Thames, Surrey,
1984–87*

*Raymond Erith and
Quinlan Terry,
doorway of Common
Room Building,
Gray's Inn, London,
1970–72*

FACING PAGE
*Raymond Erith
and Quinlan Terry,
Common Room
Building and new
Gothic buttery
attached to the exist-
ing hall on the right,
Gray's Inn, London,
1970–72*

Dufours Place

Soho, London

When Terry was confronted with a commission for an office block in Dufours Place, he could point to the experience he had gained with this type of building a decade earlier at Gray's Inn (see p. 20). Consent for development in Dufours Place had been granted on the basis of a scheme for an eight-story glass-and-concrete block, but Haslemere Estates, who had acquired the property, agreed with Terry that the time had come to show instead that it was possible to provide modern accommodation in the Georgian language. At Dufours Place, this involved adopting traditional load-bearing brick construction, rising to six stories plus attics, the maximum height that traditional construction can easily achieve. Nonetheless, it provided the same floor area as that for which permission initially had been granted. Built between 1983 and 1984, Dufours Place contains office space and twenty-five flats with cheerful red-brick exteriors, featuring white-painted, wooden sash windows, crowned by a shaped gable and jaunty cupola. The trompe l'oeil window over the main entrance provides an amusing Baroque touch, incorporating details from Ferdinando Fuga's Palazzo Corsini (1736–54), which Terry measured when in Rome.

Dufours Place, Soho, London, 1983–84

FACING PAGE
Drawing by Quinlan Terry of niche at the Palazzo Corsini, Rome (1736–54), by Ferdinando Fuga

Corsini Palace.   Niche on main stairs
Half inch scale.   1st Dec. 67

Quarter
F.S.

4. 11 1/4

Corsini Palace.
Niche on Main Stairs.

4. 1"
< to floor

Half inch scale
1st December 1867

Richmond Riverside

Richmond-on-Thames, Surrey

Dufours Place (see p. 22) led to an even larger project for the same clients at Richmond Riverside. The situation of the office buildings Terry built on the banks of the Thames at Richmond, in Surrey, helps explain their architectural character, which harmonizes with that of the riverside of Georgian London at Richmond and at nearby Twickenham and Kew. Terry's buildings are invitingly open to the river through terraces and lawns, yet they also form a group that has a powerfully urban character, surrounded by lively public streets as well as sheltering magical enclosures and squares—just the combination that visitors enjoy exploring in historic European towns and cities.

Before Terry's arrival at Richmond in 1983, a series of developers and their architects had been entangled in planning procedures for fifteen years. What was envisaged was office space capable of being rented as one or two single units to big corporate users. However, the planners of Richmond Borough Council had the unusual good sense to argue that such great blocks would be out of sympathy with the modest scale of the buildings in the heart of this historic town. They asked that the offices be brick-faced and appear to be a group of differ-ent buildings, though also requested that the same floor levels be continued throughout. Haslemere Estates agreed to buy the site on the condition that their scheme, designed by Terry along the Dufours model, would be accepted.

Instead of treating the commission as if it were one large building subdivided, Terry's scheme, built between 1984 and 1987, provided attached but separate houses with real party walls. Thus, it was not one £20M ($37.71 million) building, but twenty £1M ($1.88 million) buildings side by side. The external walls are of solid, load-bearing brickwork, stronger and more durable than all modern materials. They carry the load of the floors and the pitched roofs of Welsh slate, while the spine walls and floors are in reinforced concrete, purely to increase the net rentable area. Thus, though his buildings are in fact the individual architec-tural entities that they appear to be, they contain open-plan office accommodation, which runs counter to the suggestion of separate buildings. Further illusion is provided by their

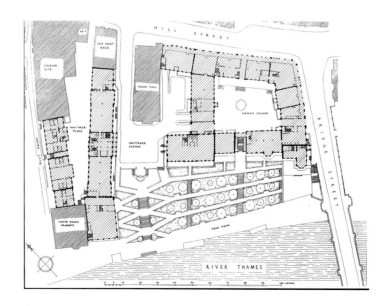

Site plan

FACING PAGE
*Restaurant building
from the River Thames*

24

TOP
Whittaker Building

BOTTOM
Elevation of Sir William Chambers design for Richmond Palace: elevation of the principal front, 1765. Pencil, pen and ink, and wash. RL29705.

Side Elevation

Plan

appearance of having grown over time, recalling traditional towns where buildings of different periods happily rub shoulders; they conform to a common vernacular, in this case, English Georgian, yet have details in different styles. The illusionist flavor enables them, in accordance with eighteenth-century picturesque theory, to evoke history through the use of past styles, while blending into their settings.

John Nash's Regent Street was built in 1815–19 not only as a property speculation but, architecturally, as a commentary on and a dialogue with the episodic picturesque grouping of the historic High Street at Oxford. He based the façade of the County Fire Office on the demolished seventeenth-century Gallery at Old Somerset House, then attributed to Inigo Jones. Examples of this technique at Richmond Riverside include Whittaker House, a stuccoed terrace of twenty-one bays that is a simpler version of an unexecuted palace design of the 1760s by Sir William Chambers and King George III. It was appropriately recalled here, for it was to have been built at Richmond. The building next to Whittaker House, planned as a restaurant, recalls an antique Roman house that Palladio unexpectedly built for the Convento della Carità in Venice (1560–74), today part of the Accademia gallery. The Palladian Venetian flavor of the restaurant suits its waterside setting, and because of the visual importance of the building, Terry was able to persuade Haslemere Estates to accept the rich Doric and Ionic stone detailing and lead roof that he proposed.

The whole development is beautifully related to the sloping site. For example, a handsome staircase leads from the Thames to Whittaker Square, flanked by zigzag ramps for wheelchair users. There are three further flights of steps rising through three levels of terraced lawns linking the buildings to the river. His frontages on Hill Street and Bridge Street feature attractive arcaded ground floors containing shops, like the historic English towns of Winchester and Chester with their Roman origins. Providing welcome shelter from the weather, the arcades boast columns in four orders: Greek Doric, Roman Doric, Tuscan, and Corinthian. Baseless columns were chosen because they allow the column height to increase down the gradient of the sloping site.

Environmental advantages of Terry's buildings are that the thick, load-bearing walls and sensibly sized windows provide interiors in which it is possible to dispense with air conditioning. Moreover, the span of the offices, twenty feet to the spine wall, which is the Georgian norm, ensures that all interior rooms are naturally lit and ventilated. Modern regulations concerning planning, building, and safety are often believed to be inimical to traditional planning, but Richmond Riverside disproves that. Even the extractor ducts for air conditioning, if required, and for the basement car-park extracts, are disguised as decorative cupolas on the roof. Finally, Richmond gave the lie to the myth that traditional buildings are more expensive than so-called "modern" ones. The cost was £80 ($151.25) per square foot, compared with over £100 ($189) for normal, air-conditioned, modern office space in central London at the time. Furthermore, most modern offices are built to last for little more than thirty years, but Terry's traditional buildings will last for generations.

Convento della Carità, Venice (1569–70), from Palladio, I Quattro Libri *(1570)*

FACING PAGE
Design for restaurant building, Richmond Riverside, Richmond-on-Thames. Drawing by Les Edwards, Rachel Canham, and Quinlan Terry, exhibited at the Royal Academy Summer Exhibition, 1987

Bedford Riverside

Bedford

Although construction at Bedford Riverside has not yet begun, it is a startling urban composition, as can be appreciated from a dramatic perspective drawing by Francis Terry. Comprising chiefly a U-sided square of shops, it has a garden sloping down to the River Ouse. This disposition recalls Richmond Riverside (see p. 24), but at Bedford the mayor and councillors also asked for a bridge with shops over the river. The elegant design of Terry's bridge has hints of Robert Adam's Pulteney Bridge at Bath (1769–74) and of Palladio's unexecuted design for the Rialto Bridge over the Grand Canal in Venice. The

south front of the main building is a monumental composition, twenty-one bays long and six stories high, with a pedimented centerpiece and crowning cupola. Below the arcaded first floor in the Doric order rise two stories of open porticoes in the Ionic and Corinthian orders. Bedford is important as an example of a provincial town seeking to emulate the success of Richmond Riverside. However, nothing has been seen with this height and scale since Adam's dramatic unexecuted designs for monumental new buildings in the center of Edinburgh.

Baker Street, Kendall Place, and George Street

London

The principles of Richmond Riverside (see p. 24) were extended to central London in Terry's important development on Baker Street, designed between 1998 and 1999 and built from 2000 to 2002. Constituting one of the largest and yet most sympathetic additions to Georgian London, it was nonetheless controversial, like so much of Terry's work. There was a twenty-year battle before permission was granted because the complete scheme involved the demolition of some minor late-eighteenth-century buildings put up by the Portman Estate. These were not considered of sufficient interest to merit listing, following evidence presented at a public inquiry into the scheme in 1996 and 1997.

The principal feature of the site was a terrace of nine late-Georgian brick houses, comprising nos. 20–36 on the east side of Baker Street, only two of which, those at the northern end, were listed. All in commercial use, these had fallen into a highly degraded condition since 1980, when the first of many schemes to redevelop the site had been rejected at a public inquiry. The buildings were sandwiched between two enormous and highly unsympathetic modern office and residential blocks to north and south. At the south end, the site turned the corner onto George Street with a further group of listed properties, and also included the west side of Kendall Place, which runs north from George Street.

Terry's scheme provided what was required by the inspector at the public inquiry and by the owner of the site, Loftus Family Property: traditional façades incorporating seven shops, a restaurant, and an impressive office reception on the first floor, with open-plan offices on the four upper floors surrounding a large atrium. In the façades of most of his new work, Terry was modest enough to echo the undemonstrative articulation of the old buildings, but for the larg-

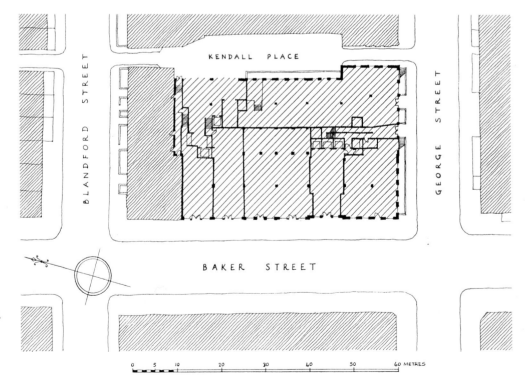

Site plan

FACING PAGE
Detail of Ionic order

FOLLOWING PAGES
View from southwest, showing new building from Blandford Street to George Street

Corner building at junction of Baker Street and George Street

er buildings at the south end with its return onto George Street, he felt it appropriate to provide the street scene with a more commanding liveliness. His corner building is thus inspired by Home House (1773–76), by Robert Adam and James Wyatt, in nearby Portman Square, while his adjacent building sports an order of giant columns rising through the two center stories. Prominence is given to this building because it contains the principal entrance and reception area to the offices that occupy a large part of the whole site. In these ways, Terry varied the details and proportions along the terrace in a picturesque manner, harking back to architects such as John Nash and to the lessons he learned from Raymond Erith in the additions at Gray's Inn (see p. 20). After he had completed his design for Baker Street, English Heritage produced photographs of four Georgian buildings on the north side of Portman Square at the junction with Baker Street, before they were demolished in 1960. It was remarkable that these included one similar to Terry's corner building with the order of giant columns.

Detail of new mews building in Kendall Place

Though Terry's designs were welcomed enthusiastically by English Heritage and by the Royal Fine Art Commission, the story did not end there, for they were opposed by planning officers at Westminster City Council in February 2000. The Georgian Group, which has a surprising record of opposition to Terry, was also unhappy. In a letter sent from the Georgian Group to Westminster in 1999, a caseworker stated that any attempt to disguise a large office block behind an elevation treated as a terrace of varied houses will be necessarily problematic. The author had evidently forgotten that architecture is the art of problem solving. Indeed, in buildings like Cumberland Terrace (1826), a few minutes away from Baker Street, Nash had solved the problem of presenting a row of houses as though they were a single palace, just as Palladio had confronted the even more challenging problem in sixteenth-century Vicenza of putting a Classical façade onto a medieval Gothic basilica.

One of the objections of the Westminster planning officers was to Terry's elevations in Kendall Place. However, this was because they had failed to grasp the difference between Kendall Place, which is a commercial mews, and some of the other mews in the Portman Conservation Area, which are traditional residential mews. "What I fear Westminster City Council has not appreciated," explained Terry in his Proof of Evidence for yet another planning inquiry, "is that for this building to be truly outstanding, the architectural priority must be the quality, appearance, and detail of the principal façades to Baker Street and George Street. Kendall Place provides the servicing and supporting role, which make the rest of the project workable and must therefore be seen as important, although subsidiary."

The scheme was finally approved in July 2000. One might have supposed that Westminster City Council would have welcomed the condition Terry exacted—that he should be allowed to build "a load-bearing solid brick construction, not a frame with a veneer of brick facing"—when he was invited to take on this commission in 1998. The high quality of these materials ensures that this is solid, enduring architecture. The walls are of load-bearing Smeed Dean or Rudgewick brown stock brick in Flemish bond set in lime mortar with rubbed and gauged brick arches; the sills, stringcourses, copings, and chimney caps are in Portland stone.

The ambitious façade with the giant Ionic order over a rusticated first floor which, as we have noted, marks the main entrance to the offices, is of Portland stone throughout. It has resonances with a range of buildings but has its origin in the richly plastic Palazzo da Porta Festa in Vicenza (ca. 1546–49), where Palladio used an engaged order for the first time. Above a rusticated first floor, Palladio's Ionic semicolumns rest directly on the stringcourse and support a tall attic story divided by deeply projecting piers. Terry's building, which also draws on the Provost's House at Trinity College in Dublin (1759), a Palladian composition by an anonymous architect, echoes many features of the Palazzo da Porto Festa. Terry also related this building to its neighbors by continuing the dentil band in the form of a plain frieze on his adjacent buildings. He enjoys this game of changing moldings in linked buildings, now simplifying them, now elaborating them. The fact that Terry's richly modeled Portland stone entrance building is smaller than the Palazzo da Porta Festa does not worry him, because near his own office in Dedham is Sherman's Hall (ca. 1735), which he characterizes as "a small building with a lot of architecture." He has made measured drawings of this enchanting building which, though only three bays wide, includes giant, Tuscan angle pilasters, round-headed and rectangular windows, a central pedimented niche flanked by fluted Ionic pilasters, and a pedimented doorcase with Corinthian pilasters in red, yellow, and gauged brickwork.

Another remarkable feature of the Baker Street development is Terry's use of stained and tuck-pointed brickwork for the large corner building at the south end. This subtle process, not normally carried out in modern work, involves filling the raked-out joints, stain-

FACING PAGE
Main entrance at 22 Baker Street

Palazzo da Porta Festa, Vicenza (1543–52), from Palladio, I Quattro Libri *(1570)*

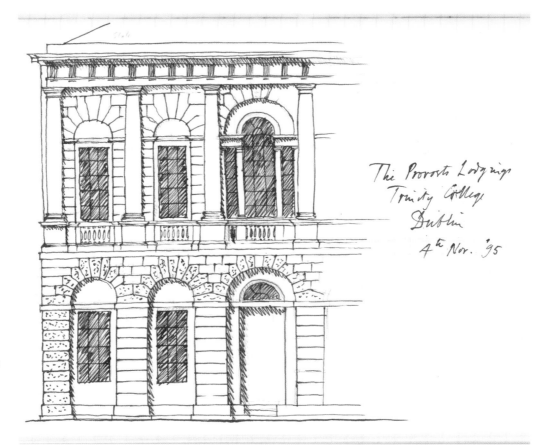

The Provosts Lodgings
Trinity College
Dublin
4th Nov. '95

Drawing by Quinlan Terry of Provost's Lodge, Trinity College, Dublin (1759)

ing the bricks and joints, and then immediately scribing a thin line at the center of the joint in lime putty to give the appearance of extremely thin jointing. Since the two surviving listed Georgian houses at the north end of the site have similar tuck pointing, the whole composition is thus balanced. All the sash windows, set in deep rendered reveals, are of custom-made hardwood sashes; the dormer windows have lead tops and cheeks; the down pipes are in cast iron with lead rainwater heads; and the roofs are Penrhyn slates. The elegant new shop fronts have windows, doors, entablatures, and pilasters in hardwood, with pilaster bases and plinths of granite.

The construction of the Baker Street development is an unusual combination of load-bearing masonry walls with a steel-framed internal structure, designed by the consultant Whitby Bird and Partners. Though this and the interiors were not designed by Quinlan Terry, the configuration should be briefly explained here since it was what made his beautiful façades possible. A central north-south corridor contains stairs, elevators, braced stability frames, and light-well, from which shallow, long-span, "Cellform" beams, containing the servicing, radiate to the masonry façades along the east, south, and west elevations. These beams support metal decking, which is then topped with a 130-millimeter (5 ⅛-inch) lightweight concrete slab. The solid, external brick walls provide lateral stability to the frame construction. However, the vital beams could not be set solidly into the façade without cracking its load-bearing masonry. Thus, an innovative pivoted connection was devised within precast bearing blocks, known on site as "construction doughnuts," which were then set into the masonry.

Property developers are reluctant to permit load-bearing masonry façades because the amount of time they take to construct delays the faster process of the erection of the steel-work and internal elements of the superstructure, with the result that at each stage the steel-

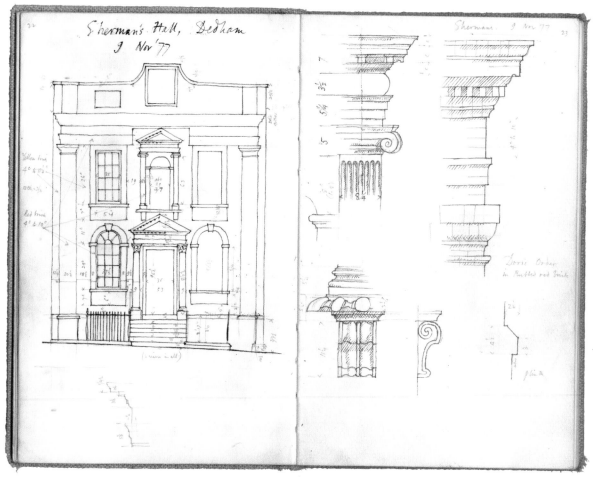

work subcontractor has to wait at every floor level for the brick laying to catch up. The building contractor, Skanska, devised a scheme in collaboration with the client and his structural engineer to enable the steel-frame erection, the concreting of the floor slabs up to the inside face of the façade, and the roof works all to be completed ahead of the construction of the façade. The permanent beams were suspended from a series of temporary steel stub columns so that, once the façade had achieved its necessary strength, the connection at the stub col-

umn was released, allowing the load to be transferred to the façade. It was thus possible to complete the frame within twelve weeks and to begin the installation of services, thereby reducing the overall construction time by at least six months—a vital consideration when costs of such magnitude are concerned.

Terry's handsome new urban composition on Baker Street has great variety of surfaces, textures, and colors as well as of forms, ranging from the elaborate use of the Ionic order to the

One of the nine carved stone plaques on the façade at Baker Street and George Street

modest façades in Kendall Place with their mews flavor, while the Georgian houses at the north end, turning the corner onto George Street, have been returned to residential use. This complex slice of London created by Terry may be welcomed as representing a kind of penance or act of reparation for the damage done by the application of Modernist principles from the 1960s in nearby Portman Square.

264-267 Tottenham Court Road

London

This project is a major intervention in the heart of commercial London and a great break-through for classical architecture—the planning inspector rejected the initial Modernist design by another architect as insufficiently in keeping with its neighbors. Terry's substantial building, providing retail office space and residential accommodation, is eleven bays long and six stories high. Commissioned by London & Regional Properties, it is on Tottenham Court Road between the Barbados High Commission and the Dominion Theatre of 1928 by W. & T. Milburn. Like some late designs by Karl Friedrich Schinkel (1781–1841), Terry's

Drawing by Martyn Winney of design for 264–267 Tottenham Court Road, London, 2005–7

building shows that a largely glass elevation, if properly articulated with the orders and with glazing bars in the windows, need not have the cold and inhuman character of other modern office blocks of glass. Its deeply modeled façade keeps the street line and relates well to the adjacent interwar, classical buildings, also of Portland stone with bronze windows. Terry's building not only restores interest and dignity to an important street that has become rather degraded but is also significant as setting a pattern for new urban developments. Completion of this project is expected in 2007.

Grosse Präsidentenstrasse

Berlin

New classical buildings have scarcely been possible in Germany after the World War II, because Hitler and his favorite architect, Albert Speer (1905–1981), adopted a German neoclassical language. This was inspired by the leading Berlin architects, Karl Friedrich Schinkel (1781–1841) and Friedrich Gilly (1772–1800), but the mistaken belief in a permanent link between particular architectural forms and politics has cast a long shadow over the use of classical forms in modern Germany. Léon Krier summed this up in a drawing inspired by the Nuremberg Trials showing a Doric column, not a Nazi, hanging from a gallows. Terry has stated that "the classical grammar remains neutral like the paint on an artist's palette." In 2002, he designed a new office building and residence in the Grosse Präsidentenstrasse in Berlin for Bernd Lunkewitz, for whom he had already built Lunkewitz House, near Frankfurt (see p. 186). Lunkewitz lamented that in rebuilding Berlin after the fall of the Berlin Wall in 1989, no attention was paid to the language of Schinkel, which had given Berlin much of its prevailing character. Regarding the new British embassy as one of the worst offenders, Lunkewitz felt that the British would have been more popular if they had had the wisdom to rebuild their old embassy, which had been bombed. Terry's office building for Lunkewitz helps compensate for the unfortunate architectural history of Berlin after unification.

It is a substantial seven-storied block, thirteen bays long, with a heavily rusticated first floor and mezzanine story immediately above it. The drawings for this are by Francis Terry, whose hand is becoming a recognizable feature of the practice. With segmentally headed windows surmounted by massive voussoirs, it echoes the language inspired by architects such as Michele Sanmicheli (1484–1559) that C. R. Cockerell devised in the 1830s to dignify the new commercial buildings required by the city of London. The crowning feature of Terry's façade is a huge cornice like that added by Michelangelo to Antonio da Sangallo's Palazzo Farnese in Rome (ca. 1530–50), while the windows below are supported by a continuous figured frieze designed by Francis Terry, depicting figures prominent in German history. This façade is characteristic of German neoclassical architecture, such as the Royal Mint in Berlin (1798–1800), designed by Heinrich Gentz with a massive frieze by Friedrich Gilly. Gentz and Gilly were the masters of Schinkel when he studied at the celebrated Bauakedemie in Berlin. The demolition of the Mint in 1886 thus represented a major loss for the city, for which Terry's new office building is in some ways a substitute.

Terry provided an alternative design for the crowning two stories, the sixth and seventh, which form a private apartment. His initial idea was for a simple block with a central canted bay and a roof garden surmounted by a balustrade, with a version of the Tower of the Winds in Athens rising from the center of the garden. The client favored a more ambitious scheme surmounted by a large belvedere in the form of a Greek Doric temple with something of the visionary character of Schinkel's celebrated unexecuted designs for the empress of Russia in 1848 for Schloss Orianda in the Crimea. At the time of this writing, it is not known which of Terry's alternative designs will be executed.

Drawing by Francis Terry of design for Grosse Präsidentenstrasse, Berlin, 2002

Merchants Square

Colonial Williamsburg, Virginia

In 2000, Quinlan Terry was given the prestigious commission for new commercial buildings at the heart of colonial Williamsburg. These were built in 2002 in Merchants Square,
near the celebrated seventeenth-century College of William and Mary. The call to work at
Williamsburg was the kind of commission that, among English architects, only Sir Edwin
Lutyens had previously achieved when he designed the British Embassy in Washington,

D.C., in 1925. Completed in 1931, his neo-Georgian embassy had features in common
with work at Williamsburg, such as the Governor's Palace, begun in 1930. The re-creation of colonial Williamsburg that began in 1926 is one of the most extraordinary in the
history of twentieth-century traditional architecture and restoration, so it was fitting that
Quinlan Terry become involved in it. He certainly appreciated the remarkable privilege

of being an English architect considered worthy by modern American architects of following in the footsteps of Sir Christopher Wren in one of the most revered places of American history.

In 1699, the legislators of Virginia decided to move the capital from Jamestown to Middle Plantation, which they renamed Williamsburg in honor of King William III of England. The plan of the new town of Williamsburg centered on Duke of Gloucester Street, the widest street in the colonies. It stretched for nearly a mile from the capitol building to the newly established College of William and Mary (1695–99). Possibly designed by the Office of the King's Works, headed by Sir Christopher Wren, the college's first building was built by English and Virginian workmen, using glass, lead, and probably ironwork imported from England, and brick, mortar, framing, and woodwork of local origin. Numerous modest private houses as well as major public buildings established Williamsburg as the political, social, and cultural center of Britain's largest and wealthiest North American colony. It filled this role until the capital was moved to Richmond during the Civil War, after which it entered a long sleep, eventually becoming thoroughly degraded with inappropriate shops, filling stations, and dominant telephone poles.

In 1926, it was reawakened by John D. Rockefeller Jr. (1874–1960), one of the most remarkable architectural benefactors of the twentieth century, who was also responsible for The Cloisters Museum in New York, the Rockefeller Museum in Jerusalem, the reconstruction of the Stoa of Attalos in Athens, and the restoration of Reims Cathedral, Versailles, and Fontainebleau in France. It was decided to restore Williamsburg not to its origins in the 1690s but to its eighteenth-century, pre-Revolutionary period. This unique re-creation of a partly lost eighteenth-century town would now, ironically, run counter to the spirit of current listed-building legislation, since it involved the demolition of more than four hundred buildings that had been added after the colonial period. Though this involved little artistic loss, the removal of a great number of attractive later additions, such as porticoes, porches, and verandas, is the occasion for mild regret.

The single most striking achievement was the complete re-creation beginning in 1930 of the palace of the royal governor of 1706, destroyed by fire in 1781. Its original appearance was known from a single modest engraving of about 1740 of one façade, from a plan drawn by Thomas Jefferson, and from excavations of the basement made in 1930. Thus, its re-creation after 1930, as I argued in *Morality and Architecture Revisited* (2001), "would now be outlawed by the modernistic rhetoric which has been increasingly adopted by bodies such as English Heritage. Their 'philosophy' would condemn the new Williamsburg for involving 'replication' based on 'insufficient historical evidence,' leading to 'inauthentic pastiche.' Certainly, about 80 percent is new . . . yet the whole is intensely beautiful and highly successful. It has become part of the American psyche and a contribution to the American understanding of its past which stimulated some of the best buildings of the colonial revival of the 1930s and 1940s."

The architects behind the restoration and reconstruction beginning in 1926 were from the Boston firm of William Perry, Thomas Shaw, and Andrew Hepburn, whose fine working drawings, which show remarkable similarities to those of Raymond Erith, are carefully stored in their archives. They introduced in front of the College of William and Mary a new commercial element named Merchants Square, built between 1929 and 1932. In 1999, the Colonial Williamsburg Foundation, the nonprofit educational organization that operates the town, decided to build a new group of shops and offices on the north side of Merchants

Detail of arched window of Corner building, showing color combination of local field brick, English rubbed and gauged brick arch with St. Bees sandstone, plinth, impost, and string course

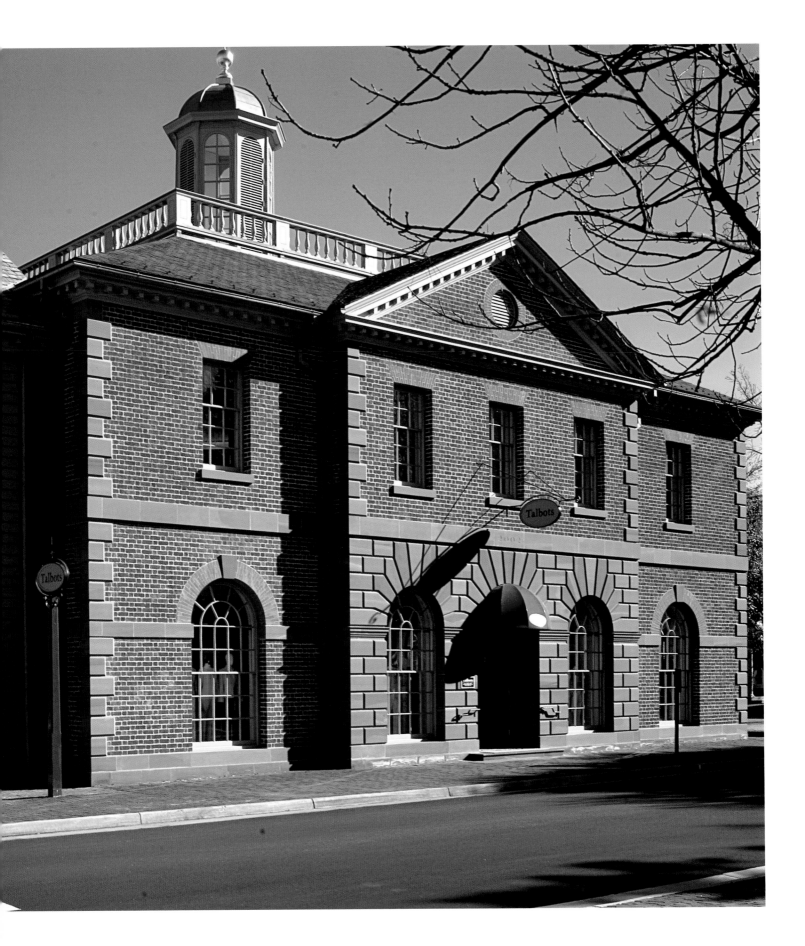

Square, on a site that had been partly occupied by an undistinguished church built in the 1920s and demolished some years ago.

Designs for this site submitted by a firm of architects from Baltimore were considered unsuitable. With the support of Colin Campbell, the newly appointed president of the Colonial Williamsburg Foundation, it was decided to take the bold step of approaching Quinlan Terry for what was to be the first substantial addition to Merchants Square since the 1930s. The foundation felt that his work at Richmond Riverside (see p. 24) showed that he was not only capable of making a major yet harmonious urban addition in a sensitive area, but that he could match the sophistication of earlier buildings at Williamsburg, such as the recreated Governor's Palace. The foundation recognized that in Terry they would have an architect with whom they could escape from the ignorant neo-Georgian work being built throughout America. In turn, he was expected to receive advice from the architects and architectural historians on the staff of the Colonial Williamsburg Foundation, particularly about historic buildings in the region.

For his buildings, Terry was able to draw on his rich knowledge of a vernacular architecture based on craftsmanship, permanent materials, and exuberant details. This was frequently an architecture without names, least of all those of the prima donna architects of the "signature buildings" of the twenty-first century. Terry looked back to English Georgian architecture for inspiration, and to local American examples such as the eighteenth-century Tidewater houses, like Rosewell on the York River and Mount Airy on the Rappahannock.

Ironically, the arrival in 2000 of Quinlan Terry, supposed archconservative, overturned the approach of previous twentieth-century architects at Williamsburg by introducing into his buildings features inspired by the late eighteenth and early nineteenth centuries. He thus dared to suggest for the first time since 1926 that Williamsburg had actually grown naturally over the years. The results can be seen in his additions to Merchants Square, currently designated the Corner Building, Middle Building, North West Building, and North East Building. Each consists of two stories and includes shops with elegant façades featuring Doric pilasters of hardwood on the first floor and office space above. The roofs are constructed of slate from Buckingham, Virginia, with lead ridges. The units into which this large group is divided are designed in different but harmonious styles and materials, one of them faced with weather-boarding, as in many of the nearby houses. This variety not only serves to reduce the apparent bulk of what is really a single construction, but also gives the impression of buildings of different dates. It is thus a perfect example of the narrative architecture of which Terry is a master, while it is also constructionally novel, combining a load-bearing masonry façade with an internal steel frame.

The most important element is the imposing Corner Building, which, resembling a public building, has one façade facing west toward the College of William and Mary and one facing south onto Merchants Square. Each front consists of five bays (the central three of which are pedimented) and is adorned with a powerfully rusticated first floor punctuated

FACING PAGE
West side of Corner building

Detail of impost molding and rustications to ground-floor window of Corner building in St. Bees sandstone

with three arched openings beneath deep voussoirs. This recalls the Town Hall at Woodstock in Oxfordshire (1766), built for the Duke of Marlborough from designs by Sir William Chambers. The rich rustication and voussoirs, sheltering windows with thin glazing bars set in deep reveals, are a pattern previously unknown in Williamsburg. However, the building also features an earlier Anglo-Dutch seventeenth-century balustraded roof-terrace surmounted by a belvedere in the form of a tall octagonal cupola, which Terry made more ambitious as the design progressed. Such a cupola had already appeared at Williamsburg on both the capitol and the Governor's Palace, while Terry had previously used this arrangement at Merks Hall in Essex (see p. 146).

Though old Williamsburg is largely brick and timber, Terry used pinkish brown sandstone from Saint Bees in Cumberland for the massive quoins, rustication, and voussoirs of the Corner Building. However, similar brown sandstone had already been used for the steps of the Court House (1770). Terry's Saint Bees sandstone was worked at the Ketton Stoneworks in Rutland and was then shipped out to Williamsburg where it was erected on site by English workmen from Ketton. The same firm thus cut and laid the stone. Current legislation prevents doors from opening out in front of the building line, but Terry made imaginative use of this by giving an exceptional depth to the arched central openings of the Corner Building. With features such as its rusticated stonework and imposing cupola, Terry's Corner Building is more powerful than the domestic buildings that line the nearby Duke of Gloucester Street, the main axial street in Williamsburg. His boldly emphatic work is made appropriate by its proximity to the College of William and Mary and the fact that its west front stands on North Boundary Street, a busy traffic artery that separates the college from Duke of Gloucester Street, which is now for pedestrians only.

Adjacent to the Corner Building on the north, and in marked contrast to it, is the modest Middle Building, in timber clapboarding. It has a truly American vernacular flavor, even though the doorcase is inspired by one in Dedham. Next to this is the North West Building in red brick, which provides another lively shift in texture and color in its rubbed brickwork combined with locally made field brick laid in Flemish bond with lime putty. With headers, stretchers, and closers all in rubbed and field bricks, it sports intricately rubbed Doric pilasters and entablatures. These were made at Lamb's brickworks in Sussex and echo East Anglian work, such as Sherman's Hall in Dedham. It is doubtful whether work of this quality has been carried out since the eighteenth century, though gauged brick had already appeared at Williamsburg on a modest scale in the Secretary's Office (1748) near the capitol. Where the North West Building meets the North East Building there is a pleasing contrast of timber, brick, and lead cornices. In contrast to Terry's other buildings, the North East Building was built with plain yellow brick from North Carolina, and has a deep cornice and hipped roof. Its Regency form is also an innovation for Williamsburg, where nothing so Regency had previously been built, or, indeed, ever proposed in Virginia, since about1810.

Bringing rubbed brickwork and Saint Bees sandstone from England was a remarkable but necessary tribute to the Old World by the New, for Modernism in America has completely destroyed the tradition in which craftsmen had been trained to produce work of this quality in brick and stone. This recalls the fact that the construction of the College of William and Mary had also, as we have seen, involved English materials and craftsmen. However, particularly in the North West Building, the skilled work of the brickmason, Raymond Cannetti, and daily supervision by the architectural historian, Edward Chappell, combined with Terry's designs to create a new standard for brickwork in the United States.

TOP
Detail of Ionic pilaster in Portland stone

BOTTOM
Niche to the center of the Northwest building showing rubbed and gauged fluted pilasters, pediment, and niche with Ionic capitals, bases, gradoons, and consoles in Portland stone

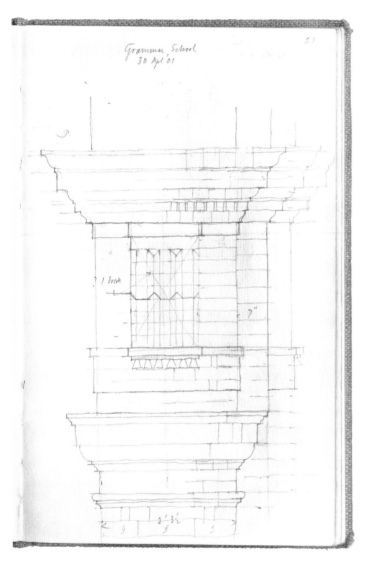

Drawing by Quinlan Terry of detail of brick entablature to the Grammar School, Dedham, Essex (ca. 1740)

Detail of rubbed and gauged Doric entablature to the Northwest building

View from the South

Quinlan & Francis Terry. Archts.
Dedham, Colchester, Essex.
March 2004

1203/6

*Drawing by Francis
Terry of first design
for Queen Mother
Square, Poundbury,
Dorset, 2004*

Queen Mother Square
Poundbury, Dorset

Poundbury is the new town begun in 1993 by the duchy of Cornwall; work is expected to be completed in about 2015. Its master plan was commissioned by the Prince of Wales from Léon Krier with the aim of re-creating traditional urbanism. The growth of out-of-town shopping centers and business parks, all heightening dependence on cars, has destroyed the sense of living in a community, as well as the commercial vitality of historic towns. Poundbury thus overthrows the zoning popular since at least the World War II, which involved separation of private from social housing and of places of work from places of residence. The rapidly growing Poundbury is already proving widely influential on modern planning.

Quinlan Terry's Queen Mother Square at Poundbury is a three-sided square with arcades of Tuscan columns and a high tower of the orders set at an angle on the northeast corner, its crowning features recalling, in one proposal, Nicholas Hawksmoor's Saint Anne's

Drawing by Quinlan Terry of Piazza del Popolo, Ascoli Piceno, Italy

Limehouse (1712–24). Another separate building on the southeast corner is arcaded on all three stories in something of the manner of Palladio's Convento della Carità in Venice. Though simple in its details, this square introduces for the first time a needed note of monumentality at Poundbury, where, in accordance with Krier's master plan, it will be the central square and focal meeting point.

Terry's square suggests the atmosphere of an outdoor drawing room, an engaging setting for daily life and conviviality. Italian towns, such as Ascoli Piceno in the Marches, similarly centered on its Piazza del Popolo (of which Terry has made drawings), are immensely popular with residents and visitors for precisely this reason. Queen Mother Square will be closed to traffic, following the example of many of the historic squares in Italian towns, including the Piazza del Popolo at Ascoli Piceno.

drawn by Francis Terry

New Infirmary, Royal Hospital
Chelsea

In 2004, Quinlan Terry was invited to provide designs for a large new infirmary on a prestigious site on the eastern side of Sir Christopher Wren's celebrated Royal Hospital at Chelsea (1682–92). These were to replace an earlier design for the building, which officers in the council-planning department found unacceptable in such a historic situation. The general principles of the internal arrangements were retained from these designs, since they were largely dictated by modern hospital requirements, but Terry provided exteriors featuring a Tuscan portico—the simplest of the orders—chosen out of deference to Wren, whose principal building at the Royal Hospital was in the nobler Doric order. Furthermore, instead of

*Drawing by Francis Terry
of first design for New
Infirmary, Royal Hospital,
Chelsea, 2005–7*

following Wren's red brick, Terry chose London stock brick, which echoes the material used by Sir John Soane for the buildings that he added on the western side of the Royal Hospital between 1809 and 1817.

As we noted in the Introduction, Terry's designs received planning consent in 2005 from all the relevant authorities, yet such is the extent of the opposition of the architectural establishment to his work that, even at this stage, leading Modernist architects sought to have the designs called in for a public inquiry. Fortunately they were unsuccessful in their desperate attempt to prevent a new public building from being built in the classical style. Work on its construction began in 2006.

CHAPTER 2

London Town Houses

Regent's Park

PREVIOUS PAGES
*Regency Villa,
Regent's Park,
London, 2000–2*

"Put on Nash's shoes and go on walking" was the challenging advice given to Quinlan Terry in 1988 by Michael Tree of the Crown Estate Commissioners when Terry was appointed architect for six new villas in Regent's Park. In John Nash's first plans for Regent's Park (1811–12), he had proposed as many as fifty-six villas, a number later cut down to twenty-six, of which only six were built in the 1820s. It was thus appropriate for the Crown Estate to consider the erection of at least six more on land in the northwest corner of Regent's Park, opposite the American Ambassador's residence, Winfield House; this land became available following the demolition of modern hostels—some built for Bedford College—that were of no architectural interest.

The site is narrow so the villas are necessarily close to the Outer Circle, the road that runs around the park. However, at the rear, the land slopes steeply down on the northwest side to the extremely attractive Regent's (now Grand Union) Canal, laid out by Nash from 1811 to 1820 as part of the Grand Union Canal connecting Paddington with the new docks on the Isle of Dogs. Terry therefore designed the villas with their most commanding elevations on this side, where they can be viewed from the canal and the towpath that runs along it, as well as from Nash's Macclesfield Bridge, which crosses the canal at this point. Constituting one of the most picturesque if least known sights of London, the scene that Terry created recalls the Brenta Canal, which is also lined with villas as it approaches Venice from Padua.

Because of their commanding views to the northwest over the canal, Terry gave all the villas a similar plan with a generous loggia in the middle of the garden front. This opens onto a paved and balustraded terrace approached by great stone staircases, below which terraced gardens supported on walls paneled with flint descend to the canal. He took as guidance for his plans those of the villas built by Palladio in the Veneto. Although as few as eight drawings are typically needed for the ordinary modern house, Terry's office prepared as many as three hundred drawings for each of his villas in Regent's Park, so that the builders and craftsmen had detailed patterns to follow at every turn.

Terry's Regent's Park villas are built of two thick skins of nine-inch, load-bearing brickwork, faced in stucco, with dressings in both natural and reconstructed stone. There is local precedent for this choice in the form of Nash's terraces, which are also faced with stucco, while the ancient Romans offer a precedent for the use of reconstructed stone. They had developed a form of reconstructed stone—a version of concrete—by binding together fragments of broken stone with a mortar of lime and *pozzuolana* (volcanic ash). Modern reconstructed stone is real stone crushed and remolded in the interests of economy, although the best reconstructed stone is scarcely cheaper than natural stone. Its quality has improved, partly because architects as prolific and exacting as Quinlan Terry have chosen to use it. According to Terry, it has approached the quality of eighteenth-century Coade stone. He finds it useful to make molds if a feature is repeated many times, as in the constituent parts of balustrades; however, he prefers to use real stone when just one or two highly crafted details are needed. Terry considers reconstructed Portland stone aesthetically more acceptable than reconstructed Northamptonshire limestones, such as Clipsham or Ketton, which contain glistening minerals that tend to be lost in the process

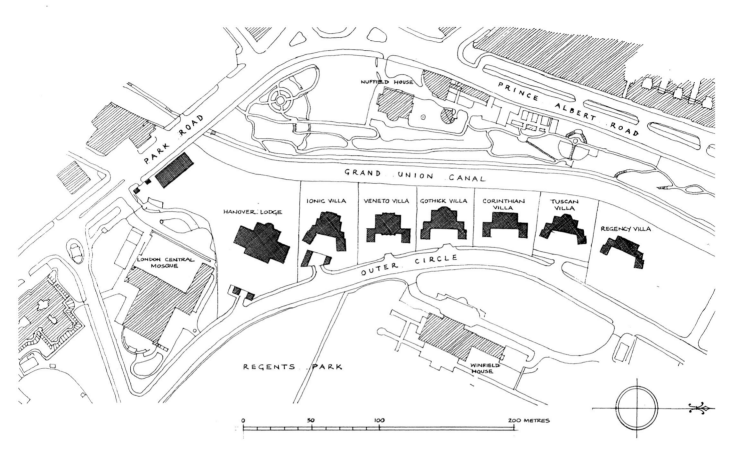

Villas in Regent's Park, London, site plan

of reconstruction. Portland stone, by contrast, can appear rather dull and gray even when natural.

Terry's first three villas at Regent's Park, named the Ionic Villa, Veneto Villa, and Gothick Villa, are not neo-Nash in style but are rich both externally and internally with resonances of English and Italian architecture from the mid-sixteenth to the early nineteenth centuries—that is to say, from Palladio to John Nash. Adding greatly to the scenic exuberance and variety of Nash's Regent's Park, they set up a range of stimulating associations, backward and forward in time, like Nash's own architecture.

IONIC VILLA

The first of the new villas built at Regent's Park, Ionic Villa (1988–90), is next door to Hanover Lodge (see p. 112). Since it is at the broadest end of the whole site of the new villas, Terry believed it should have a narrow front but greater depth than the adjacent villas. He found a useful model for its plan in that of a villa, three rooms deep, published by Palladio in his *Quattro Libri dell'Architettura*. Designed in about 1553 for Signor Girolamo Ragona from Vicenza for his estate at Ghizzole, it is uncertain whether the Villa Ragona was ever built.

Terry follows the typical 1-3-1 bay division of the entrance façade of the Villa Ragona, where the three central bays consist of a four-columned portico. Terry switches the order from Palladio's Corinthian to a simpler Ionic and, in view of the English climate, engages the columns to the solid wall, rather than opening up the portico to the interior space as in Palladio's plan. The rich details of Terry's portico repay careful study because they do justice to the full Ionic order, as set out by Palladio elsewhere in *I Quattro Libri*. They include enrichments such as bead-and-reel moldings in the capitals and entablature, and coffers containing rosettes in the modillions of the cornice and pediment. Vigorously carved from designs by Quinlan Terry's son, Francis, the coat of arms, with elephants as magnificent supporters, of Lord Bagri, the purchaser of the villa, fills a cartouche in the pediment.

The Ionic Villa is approached through a small forecourt paved with granite setts, which, since the Outer Circle follows a natural curve, is set at an angle to the villa. Terry has created a theatrical approach guarded by a pair of hexagonal piers with vermiculated rustication supporting ambitious urns. These are linked through railings around the forecourt to the actual entrance gates, which are centered on the front door. Modest, one-storied service wings set at a slight angle to the entrance front flank the villa. Since the original purchase of the villa from the Crown Estates by the Bagri family, Terry has twice enlarged it, including

Villa Ragona (ca.1553), from Palladio, I Quattro Libri *(1570)*

FACING PAGE
Entrance front

FOLLOWING PAGES
Entrance front and gate piers with wings added in 2002

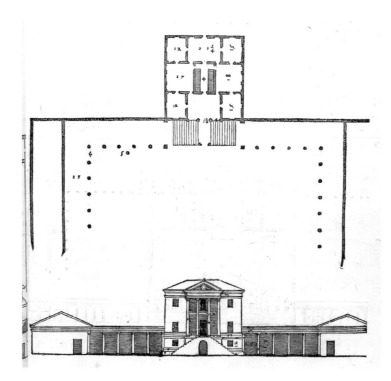

66

The Customs House
Kings Lynn
13th Sept '90

48

LEFT
*Drawing by Quinlan Terry of
the Customs House, Kings Lynn,
Norfolk (1683)*

FACING PAGE
View from the Grand Union Canal

the remodeling of the forecourt in 2002 by the addition of two further canted wings to the east and west. Also set at an angle, these create a sense of false perspective, which emphasizes the lively, stage-set character of the approach.

Comparing the plan of the Ionic Villa with that of the Villa Ragona, we are reminded that Quinlan Terry never blindly follows any source but rather creates his own achievement out of the past. Indeed, his master and former partner, Raymond Erith, was so conscious of the intensively creative work involved in the handling of historic resonances that he was reluctant ever to mention the range of his sources for fear of suggesting that it involved a simple process of copying. While Villa Ragona was planned with a centrally placed rectangular hall containing a staircase rising in two, straight, parallel flights, the more poetic, centrally placed hall at the Ionic Villa is oval in plan, with cantilevered stairs following the curve of the outer walls. It is also dramatically top-lit by a prominent cupola, rising above an external balustraded platform that follows a familiar Anglo-Dutch, seventeenth-century type, as at the Customs House at King's Lynn in Norfolk (1683). Nonetheless, Terry's staircase has an elegant neoclassical flavor, with walls in golden yellow, Siena-marble scagliola, as in the staircase hall of Sir John Soane's Museum. Soane is also recalled in the crisp design of the cast-iron balustrade.

Palladio is the most widely imitated architect in history partly because he devised a universally acceptable domestic plan, which has been capable of adaptation in different circumstances for the last four and a half centuries since its forms were not determined by technology. Terry describes it as a sensible "noughts and crosses" disposition with no wasteful corridors. Thus, at the Ionic Villa, a hall three windows wide leads into the dining room, staircase, and drawing room, all of which lead into the loggia on the garden front. This leaves four spaces in the corners of the plan for a sitting room, study, pantry, and lavatory. The house is notable for its sumptuous finishing, notably the polychromatic marble floors in geometric patterns, which have replaced the original simpler floors at the request of the patrons. The hall and staircase, as well as all the door surrounds, repay careful study.

VENETO VILLA

For the plan of the Veneto Villa (1989–91), where the site allowed a wider frontage than for the Ionic Villa, Palladio's Villa Badoer (1554) and Villa Zeno (ca. 1554), which are three bays deep and three bays wide, provided inspiration. Terry's animated two-storied façade with superimposed orders—Doric on the first floor with Ionic above—contrasts strikingly with the single giant Ionic order of the villa next door. Terry was familiar with the superimposition of these orders from his experience with the main façade of King's Walden Bury (see p. 140), on which he worked with Raymond Erith. The rich, two-tiered, façade of the Veneto Villa was also inspired by the Cornaro Loggia in Padua (1524) by Giovanni Maria Falconetto, which appealed to Terry as an ideal background for the theatrical performances popular in the Veneto. Other Palladian themes at the Veneto Villa include the variation at the ends of the façade between circular column shafts and fluted pilasters with breaks for projections, the whole composition determined by the spacing of the triglyphs and metopes on the first floor, and the use of modillions in the Ionic order above.

The internal detail, though English, displays a strong Veneto flavor in the joisted ceilings, Doric-pilastered drawing room, and stone and marble floors and chimneypieces. Employment has been given to craftsmen in wood, plaster, iron, stucco, marble, and stone, while there is also decorative graining on soft-wood doors and bookcases in a brilliant simulation of oak. An Italian sculptor from Pisa carved the Carrara-marble chimneypiece in the dining room, with its beautiful heads based on figures by the Sicilian Baroque stuccoist, Giacomo Serpotta (1656–1732). In the design of the floors, Terry was inspired by that of the floor in the monks' choir at Palladio's San Giorgio Maggiore in Venice (1564–80).

Drawing by Francis Terry of the Cornaro Loggia, Padua (1524), by Giovanni Maria Falconetto

*View from the
Grand Union Canal*

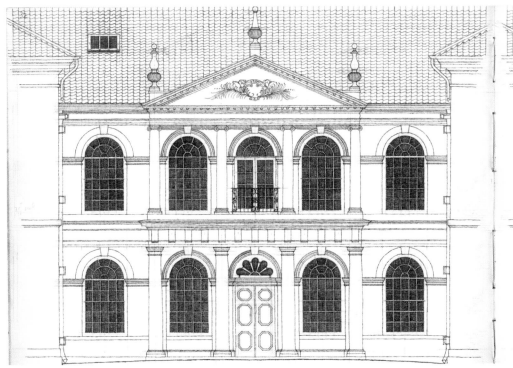

*Drawing by Quinlan
Terry of the entrance
front of King's
Walden Bury,
Hertfordshire*

FOLLOWING PAGES
*Entrance front seen
through the gate piers*

75

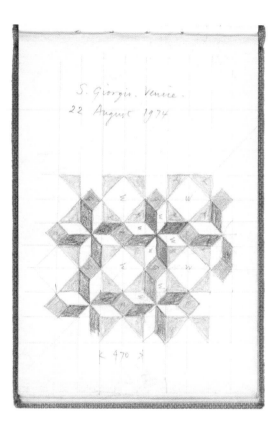

ABOVE
*Drawing by Quinlan
Terry of floor in
S. Giorgio Maggiore,
Venice (1564–80),
by Palladio*

RIGHT
Loggia

GOTHICK VILLA

The Gothick Villa (1989–91), on a narrower site, was inspired by Palladio's Villa Saraceno (1548–49), which is two rooms deep. It was a pleasing conceit to give this villa a Gothic façade and interior detailing as a tribute to Nash's own numerous Gothic buildings such as Longner Hall in Shropshire (1803), though Terry also notes that he was following "the Venetian precedent of a Classical plan with Gothic treatment." The Gothic references derive from sources such as James Gibbs's Temple of Liberty at Stowe (1741) and Batty Langley's Gothic orders, while the details follow Terry's measurements of early-nineteenth-century work at Combermere Abbey in Cheshire, on which he worked with Raymond Erith in 1972.

In the hall of the Gothick Villa is an arcade of ogee arches in Sicilian marble carved by craftsmen from Forte dei Marmi, near Viareggio. The lozenge-patterned floor derives from that in a mosque in Cairo and is laid with Portland, York, Black, and Westmoreland Green slate. The Byzantine capitals, inspired by those in the Dome of the Rock in Jerusalem, are carved with acanthus leaves rising from basketwork, in reference to the account by Vitruvius of the origin of the Corinthian order. According to Vitruvius's story, the sculptor Callimachus came upon a basket containing the favorite possessions of a young girl from Corinth, which, covered with a roof tile and placed on her tomb, had become overgrown with the leaves and stalks of an acanthus plant. By the seventeenth century, Fréart de Chambray and Claude Perrault had both published drawings illustrating this story but had not carried them into execution.

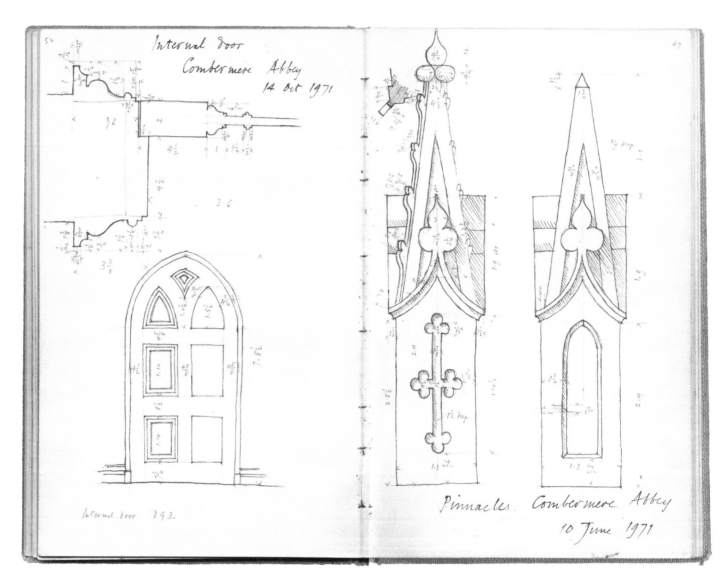

ABOVE
*Drawings by Quinlan Terry of
details at Combermere Abbey,
Cheshire (ca. 1810)*

FACING PAGE
Staircase hall, Gothick Villa

CL

CAPITAL CONSTRUCTED FROM WHITE MARBLE.
(APPROVED)

L8 RADIUS

POLISHED COLUMN SHAFT

STONE JOINT

110

SECTION THROUGH CENTRE LINE

ELEVATION OF CAPITAL

*Drawing by Francis Terry of capital
for entrance hall, based on the
Byzantine capital at the Dome
of the Rock, Jerusalem*

Capital in entrance hall

CORINTHIAN VILLA

Terry was commissioned by a private client in 2001 to build the designs he had previously prepared for three other villas for the Crown Estate Commissioners: the Corinthian Villa, Tuscan Villa (see p. 104), and Regency Villa (see p. 110). However, the three new villas are larger than they seem, for the sloping site allows for extensive basement areas including offices, services, and handsome swimming pools. Terry believes the Corinthian Villa, envis-

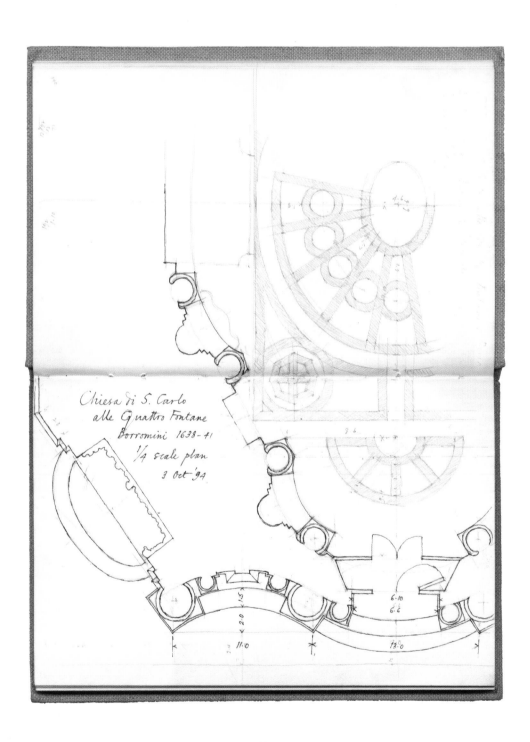

Drawing by Quinlan Terry of plan of S. Carlo alle Quattro Fontane, Rome (1665–67), by Borromini

FACING PAGE
Entrance front

aged as early as 1990, marks a turning point in his career because it demonstrates his growing belief that the forms and ornaments of the Italian Baroque can be incorporated into the Palladian tradition with which much of his work has been associated. In early-eighteenth-century England, Thomas Archer (1668–1743) and Francis Smith (1672–1738) of Warwick borrowed individual decorative motifs from Baroque Italy, such as false perspective window surrounds. But at the Corinthian Villa, Quinlan Terry goes beyond this, adopting the forms pioneered by Borromini, who set walls in motion through the use of swinging forms, curves, and counter-curves in façades such as that of San Carlo alle Quattro Fontane in Rome (designed in the 1630s; built 1665–67). Terry was, remarkably, the first architect to do this

in the history of English architecture, though such forms had spread from Italy to Germany and central Europe in the eighteenth century. Terry wonders whether architects like Francis Smith and James Gibbs (1682–1754) might have gone further in the language of Borromini but for the condemnation of Italian Baroque as "affected and licentious" and somehow unclassical in *Vitruvius Britannicus* (1715) by Colen Campbell (1676–1729) who, with Lord Burlington (1694–1753), promoted the revival of a rather dry form of Palladianism.

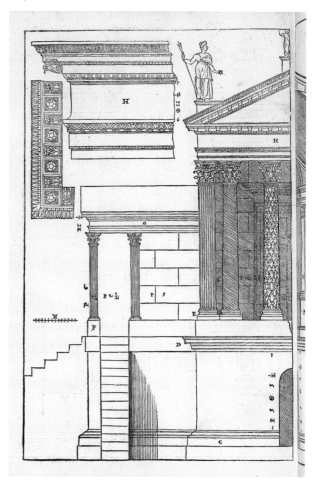

The Corinthian Villa remains, however, a four-square English house behind its undulating façade, and is far from a copy of any building by Borromini. For example, Terry's undulating architrave of reconstructed stone rests on columns of Portland stone that are hand-carved with spiral fluting, a form found in the fifth-century Temple of Clitumnus, recorded by Palladio, and in Sanmicheli's richly ornamental buildings in Verona, the Palazzo Bevilacqua (ca. 1530) and the Cappella Pellegrini at San Bernardino (1527–1557). Further lavish rich ornament is provided by the elaborately carved bases of Quinlan Terry's columns, which are inspired by those in the Baptistery of Constantine (ca. 315–324 A.D.) at Saint John Lateran in Rome. The Baptistery was illustrated by Palladio in Book IV of *I Quattro Libri dell'Architettura*, devoted to antique buildings in Rome and elsewhere. This building had

attracted Terry's attention as early as 1967 or 1968 during his stay in Rome, where he made measured drawings of its unusual order, noting that Palladio's records of the capitals were inaccurate.

FACING PAGE
Detail of entrance front

ABOVE
Temple of Clitumnus, near Spoleto, Italy (fourth century AD), from Palladio, I Quattro Libri *(1570)*

The bases of the columns in the Baptistery have elaborately carved torus moldings, above which are unusally placed carvings of tall leaves that support the column shafts. Palladio explained how he had borrowed these forms "for the columns, which I placed as ornaments at the door of San Giorgio Maggiore in Venice." Such highly ornamental work was not, in general, the aspect of Palladio that appealed to the more austere tastes of Campbell, Burlington, and their followers, who constructed an influential, if limited, image of Palladio. This ignored his rich, even mannerist late works of the 1560s, such as the Villa Barbaro at Maser (1549–58) and the Palazzo Valmarana at Vicenza (1566–72). Terry is thus

Palazzo Bevilacqua, Verona (ca. 1530), engraving by Francesco Ronzani and Girolamo Luciolli, Le fabbriche . . . di Michele Sanmicheli *(1832)*

influenced by a rounder vision of Palladio than that of the neo-Palladianism of eighteenth-century Britain.

The spiral-fluted columns of the Corinthian Villa have capitals of a richness that matches that of their bases; they are based on drawings by Francis Terry of the celebrated story told by Vitruvius of the origin of the form and ornament of the Corinthian capital. A version of this capital had already appeared, as we have noted, in the arcade in the hall of the Gothick Villa (see p. 80).

In constructing such capitals at the Corinthian Villa, Francis Terry has introduced a striking innovation of his own by inverting the volutes so that they curve downward, not upward. In this new rhythm, his intertwining plant forms are set against a deeply cut basket-work pattern, while the frieze between the capitals is carved with rich swags of fruit and ornamental ribbons, recalling a similar disposition seen at Palladio's San Giorgio Maggiore in Venice, drawn by Quinlan Terry in 1985. The ambitious staircase on the garden front of the Corinthian Villa has curvaceous and closely spaced balustrades, which echo those in the chapels that Borromini rebuilt at Saint John Lateran in Rome (1646–56), where the balusters are set alternately with their pointed edges and their flat sides forward.

Terry's fascination with Baroque form and freedom in churches like Santa Maria Maddalena in Rome (1668–71) appeared increasingly frequently in his sketchbooks, almost to the exclusion of other styles. These churches became the new focus of travels in Bavaria and

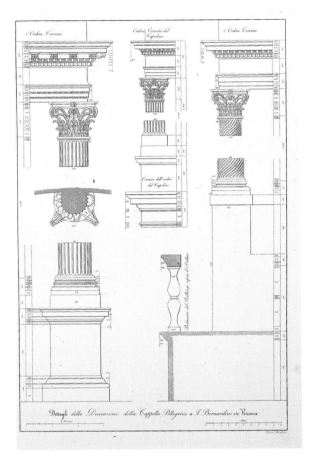

Italy. He spent three days in Syracuse with his son, Francis, drawing the eighteenth-century Baroque façades of San Francesco (the Immaculata), with its double S-curve, and of the Duomo, admiring the way it ruthlessly covered over the Greek temple behind it. Considering his work in comparison to this Baroque masterpiece, he felt deprived and longed for an opportunity to move classical detail in a Baroque direction; the Corinthian Villa gave him this chance.

Moreover, while working on the designs in 2004 for Miramar, a house in Dallas, Terry became increasingly aware that English architects from Inigo Jones (1573–1652) onward, as well as their American followers, generally took from Palladio those elements that they understood and with which they sympathized, notably his system for proportions, use of the orders, and refined detail, and sought purity in him, overlooking the element of fantasy that entered his work in about 1560. This can be found in the richly molded wall masses of his sculpturally decorated Villa Barbaro at Maser and Loggia del Capitaniato in Vicenza (1571), with its overscaled mannerist triglyphs; in the Palazzo Valmarana in Vicenza, its layered façade unusually terminated by caryatids; in the lively open oculi derived from Bramante that appear at his Villa Poiana in Poiana Maggiore (ca. 1545) and elsewhere; and in his playful use of perspective. Architects of the Palladian Revival also ignored the ebullient yet scholarly departures in his work, which were based on his study of the ornamental side of antique and later architecture. These included his measurements of the Temple of Clitumnus, of Byzantine detail, and of the Early Christian Baptistery of Constantine at Saint John Lateran.

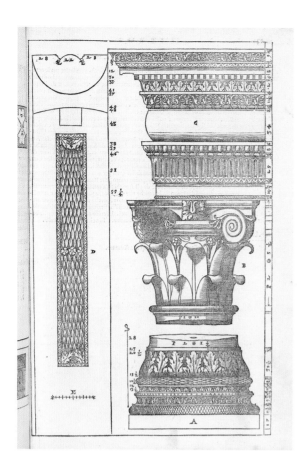

LEFT
Baptistery of Constantine, St. John Lateran, Rome (ca. 315–24 AD), from Palladio, I Quattro Libri (1570)

BELOW
Drawing by Francis Terry of the origins of the Corinthian order

FACING PAGE
Drawings by Quinlan Terry of the order of the Baptistery of Constantine, St. John Lateran, Rome (ca. 315–24 AD)

la Regent's Park, London

a certain **Corinthian** girl, just old enough to think of marriage, fell ill and died. After the funeral her nurse gathered into a basket the pots and cups which the girl had liked most when she was alive, carried them to the monument and put the basket on top of it. She covered the basket with a tile so things might survive that much longer than if they had just been put out in the open air. By chance she had placed the basket right over an acanthus root which, being pressed down by the weight, put out rather stunted leaves and shoots next spring. The shoots clung to the sides of the basket as they grew and since they were pressed down by the weight of the tile - were forced into curves and volutes at the corners. Callimachus, who for the elegance and refinement of his carving in marble was called 'catatechnos' by the Athenians, passed by the monument just then and noticed the basket and the tender leaves. Pleased with the whole thing and the novel shape, he made some columns for the Corinthians based on this model and fixed the canon of their proportion

Vitruvius bk IV, ch 1

Quinlan Terry Arch.

Francis Terry delt.

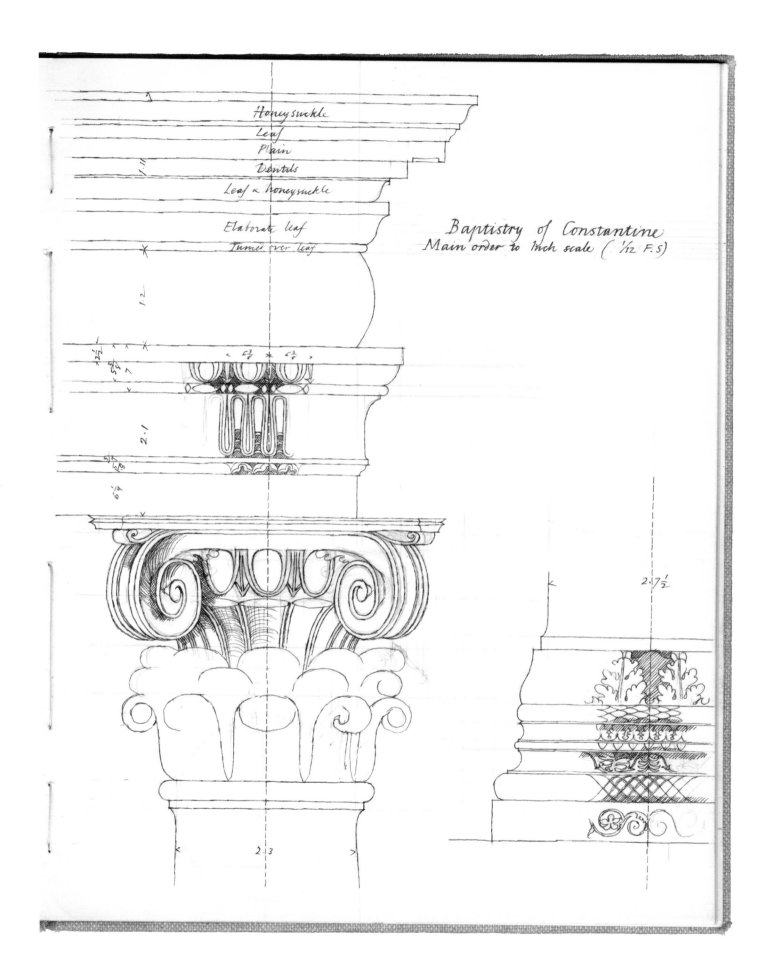

Honeysuckle
Leaf
Plain
Dentils
Leaf & honeysuckle

Elaborate leaf
Turned over leaf

Baptistry of Constantine
Main order to Inch scale (1/12 F.S)

95

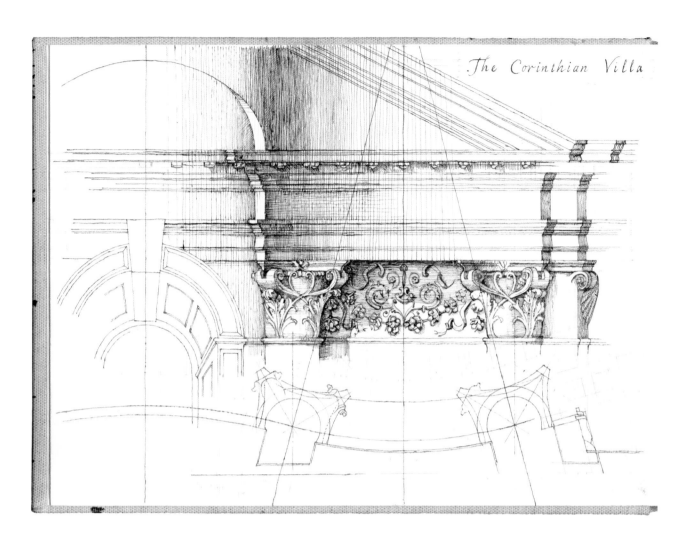

PREVIOUS PAGES
PAGE 94
*Details of capitals, swag, and entablature
to the south front, Corinthian Villa*

PAGE 95, TOP
*Drawing by Francis Terry of capitals
and entablature, Corinthian Villa*

PAGE 95, BOTTOM
*Drawing by Francis Terry of swag,
Corinthian Villa*

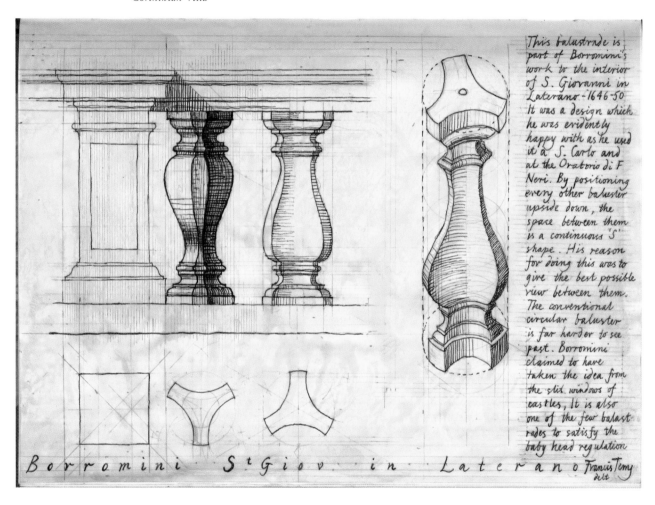

This balustrade is part of Borromini's work to the interior of S. Giovanni in Laterano - 1646-50 It was a design which he was evidently happy with as he used it a S. Carlo and at the Oratorio di F Neri. By positioning every other baluster upside down, the space between them is a continuous 'S' shape. His reason for doing this was to give the best possible view between them. The conventional circular baluster is far harder to see past. Borromini claimed to have taken the idea from the slit windows of castles, It is also one of the few balastrades to satisfy the baby head regulation

Borromini St Giov in Laterano   *Francis Terry delt*

ABOVE
*Drawing by Francis Terry of balustrade
(1646–50) by Borromini at St. John Lateran,
Rome*

FACING PAGE
Canal front, Corinthian Villa

Reproduced in this book are drawings by Terry of Baroque buildings, including the rich façade of the Duomo at Syracuse (1724–58) with its broken segmental pediment, built from designs by Andrea Palma; churches in Rome by Borromini, Carlo Rainaldi (1611–1691), and Giuseppe Sardi (1680–1753); and the broken pediments of Baldassare Longhena's staircase at San Giorgio Maggiore in Venice (1643–45). Such work was dismissed in England as irrational or worse from the time of Colen Campbell in the early eighteenth century until the rehabilitation of the Baroque in the 1920s. In other drawings of Italian sixteenth-century buildings, Terry records the mannerist tabernacle frames of the Porta Pia in Rome (1562) by Michelangelo; the elaborately detailed columns of Sanmicheli's Palazzo Bevilacqua and Cappella Pellegrini at San Bernardino in Verona; and Palladio's Loggia del Capitaniato in Vicenza. The exuberant, almost Baroque character of the Loggia del Capitaniato reminds one that Palladio was an exceptionally innovative architect as well as a very imitative one, with a readiness to learn from the past; he was content to write of his Convento della Carità in Venice that, "I endeavored to make this house like those of the ancients." By a further twist, he was probably also the most imitated architect in history.

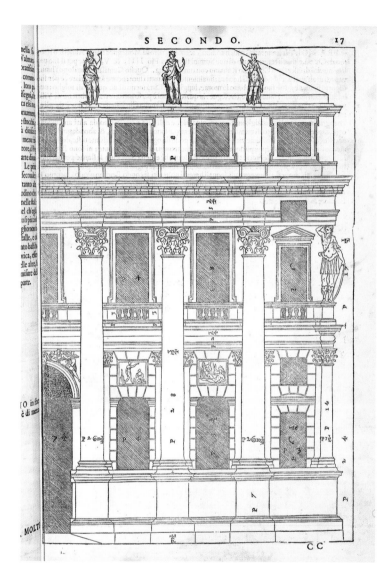

Palazzo Valmarana, Vicenza (1565–72), from Palladio, I Quattro Libri *(1570)*

FACING PAGE
Drawing by Quinlan Terry of the façade (1728) by Andrea Palma of the Duomo, Syracuse

For Terry's Corinthian Villa and its off-spring, Fristling Hall, he was assisted by his 1994 drawings of Borromini's San Carlo alle Quattro Fontane, and his 1987 drawings of Santa Maria Maddalena in Rome, with its concave Rococo façade of 1735 by Sardi, which he has long found exciting. At Terry's Fawley House in Oxfordshire (see p. 190), the incorporation of a segmental pediment within a triangular one recalls his drawing of the complex façade of Santa Maria in Campitelli in Rome (1663–67) by Rainaldi. Furthermore, Terry's magnificent gates at Foliejon Park (see p. 172) have a height and an exuberance that are positively Baroque.

Francis Terry, whose rich drawing style has contributed to the Baroque decorative style of the Terry partnership, has drawn Borromini's balustrade at Saint John Lateran in Rome, adding a note to explain that alternate balusters are upside down, a Baroque spatial device that opens up views between them, in contrast to circular balusters, which are less easy to see past. As Quinlan Terry observed in 2004, "As architects get older and wiser they tend to move in a Baroque direction." That was certainly a path he adopted in his designs for a vast domed mansion in New Delhi for Ajay Kalsi. Its X-plan is inspired by Filippo Juvarra's dynamic royal hunting lodge, Stupinigi (1729–33), near Turin.

Il Duomo. Siracuse
30 Sept 1992
Arch. Andrea di Palma
1754

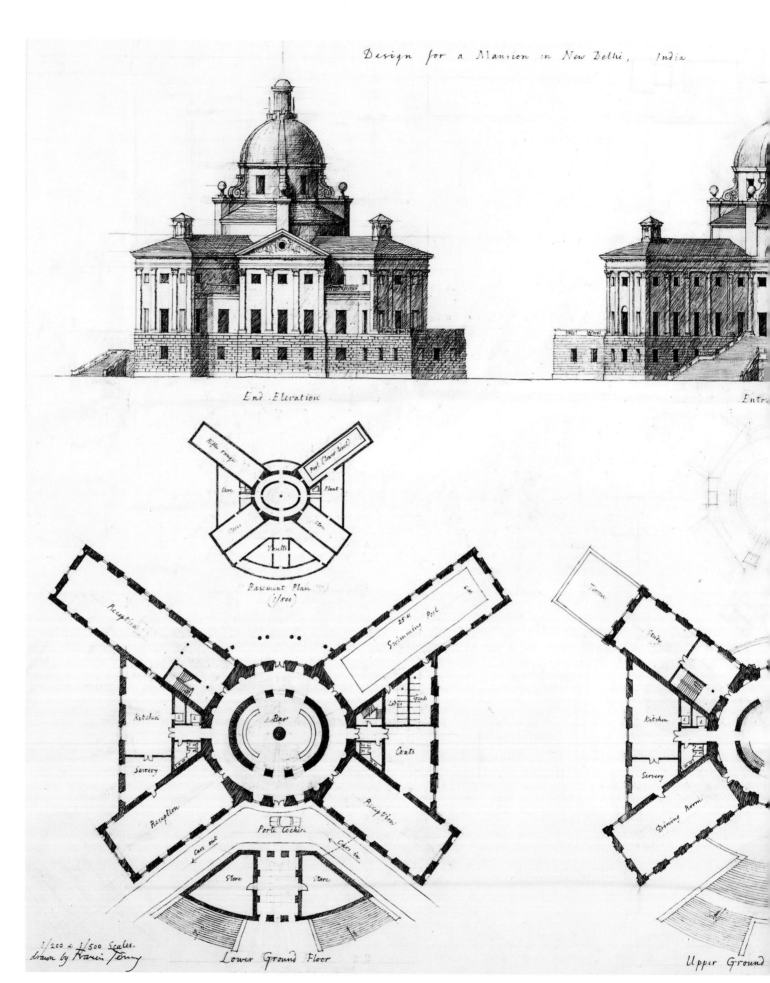

Design for a Mansion in New Delhi, India

End Elevation

Entra

Rifle range

Pool (lower level)

Store

Plant

Store

Stores

Vaults

Basement Plan
(1/500)

Reception

Kitchen

25 m
Swimming Pool

6 m

Scullery

Ladies

Gents

Coats

Reception

Bar

Reception

Porte Cochère

Cars out

Cars in

Store

Store

1/200 & 1/500 Scales.
drawn by Francis Terry

Lower Ground Floor

Terrace

Study

Kitchen

Scullery

Dining Room

Upper Ground

*Drawings by Francis Terry of plans,
elevations, and section of proposed
mansion in New Delhi, 1995*

102

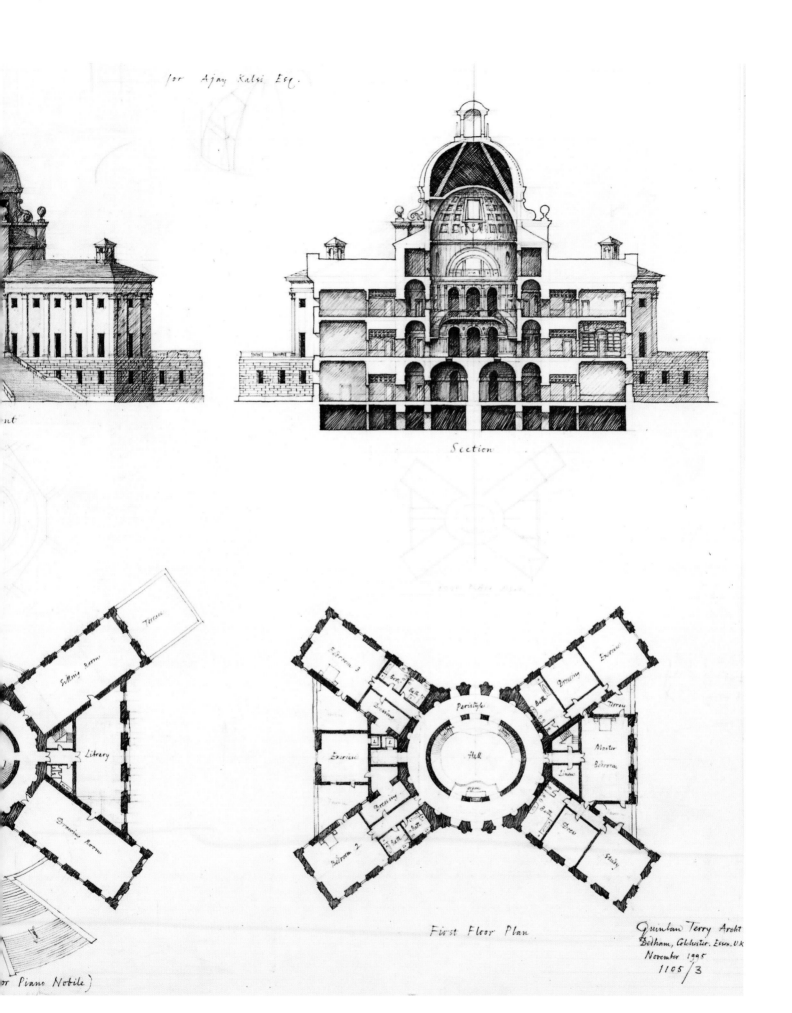

for Ajay Kalsi Esq.

Section

nt

First Floor Plan

Quinlan Terry Archt
Dedham, Colchester. Essex. U.K
November 1995
1105/3

or Piano Nobile)

TUSCAN VILLA

The Tuscan Villa was designed as Terry's response to one of the most elegant villas in London, Asgill House in Richmond (1761–64), by Sir Robert Taylor. Asgill House is a bold composition, admirably suited to its eye-catching site above the River Thames by Richmond Bridge, where it can, as it were, both see and be seen. Occupying a similarly enviable position above the Regent's Canal, the Tuscan Villa echoes the form of Asgill House, with its three-bay canted center flanked by two-storied wings, its balustrades below the second-floor

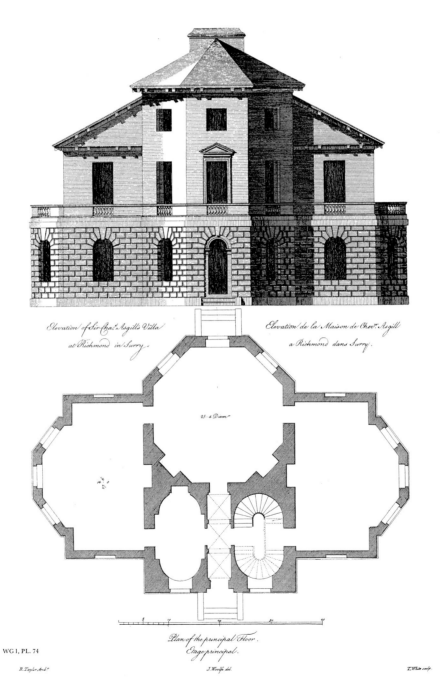

Elevation of Sir Cha⁵ Asgill's Villa   Elevation de la Maison de Chev⁵ Asgill
at Richmond in Surry.   a Richmond dans Surry.

Asgill House, Richmond, Surrey (1761–64), by Sir Robert Taylor, elevation and plan, from Vitruvius Britannicus, *vol. IV, 1767*

FACING PAGE
Entrance front, Tuscan Villa

WG I, PL. 74

R. Taylor Arch⁵   J. Woolfe del.   T. White sculp.

Plan of the principal Floor.
Etage principal.

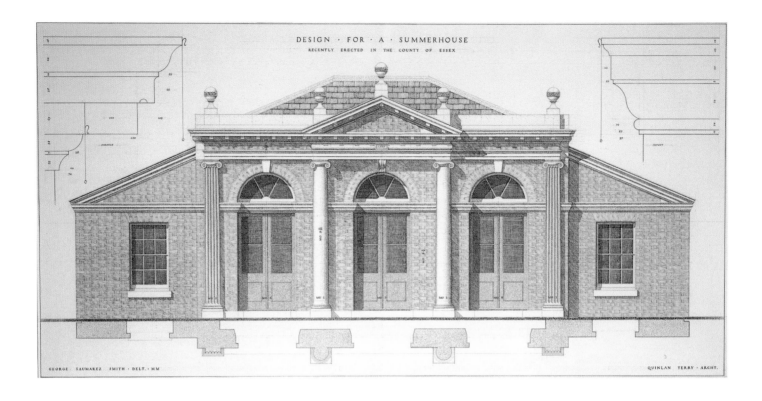

GEORGE SAUMAREZ SMITH · DELT · MM   QUINLAN TERRY · ARCHT.

Drawing by George Saumarez Smith of design for summer house, Terling Place, Essex, 1998

FACING PAGE
Summer house, Terling Place, Essex, 1998

windows, and its rusticated first floor. The Tuscan theme that appears in the projecting eaves of Asgill House is paralleled in Terry's Tuscan Villa by the prominent entrance door flanked by Tuscan columns. In adopting the Tuscan order, Terry was influenced by the distinguished precedent of Inigo Jones at Saint Paul's in Covent Garden (1631–33).

Terry's entrance front also recalls the two pediments, a larger and a smaller one, by which Palladio created the illusion of two superimposed temple fronts at his Venetian churches. This was Palladio's solution to the problem of applying a classical temple front to a church that required a nave and aisles, a device perhaps inspired by Vitruvius's account of the basilica and temple that he built at Fano, and which Palladio illustrated in Daniele Barbaro's edition of Vitruvius's *De Architectura* (1567).

Quinlan Terry had already employed this form on a small scale in his elegant summer house for Lord Rayleigh at Terling Place in Essex (1998), while he was also aware of another Sir Robert Taylor precedent in the fishing temple that Taylor had built in about 1760 at Tendring Hall, not far from Terry's office in Dedham. Terry had also used this form on a small scale in his houses at Frog Meadow in Dedham, built in 1979.

LEFT
Drawing by Francis Terry of
Fishing Temple, Stoke-by-Nayland,
Suffolk (ca.1750–60), attributed to
Sir Robert Taylor

BELOW
St. Paul, Covent Garden, London
(1631–33), by Inigo Jones, from
Vitruvius Britannicus, *vol. II,*
1717

FACING PAGE
p. 107 Detail of balcony,
Tuscan Villa

REGENCY VILLA

The Regency Villa is a powerful essay in Greek Doric and would have been called the Doric Villa but for the existence of a pair of houses of that name that Nash built next to York Terrace. In fact, the four-square, blocky forms of the Regency Villa are more characteristic of the bold, neoclassical architecture of Schinkel in Germany than of English Regency design. The beautiful figure carvings in the metopes of the Doric frieze are based on drawings by Francis Terry of Hellenistic sculpture in the British Museum. The Greek Doric columns on the entrance front are engaged, but those on the garden front form a massive open portico of free-standing columns of solid masonry construction. Normally, one would expect the grander portico to be on the front elevation, but, once again, because of the unusual site, the most dominant feature is placed at the rear.

Drawing by Francis Terry of metope in the Doric frieze

FACING PAGE
Detail of entrance façade

HANOVER LODGE

In 1995, Terry prepared designs for the rebuilding and restoration of Hanover Lodge, next door to the Ionic Villa. Built in about 1827 by Decimus Burton, Hanover Lodge was never one of the more interesting features of Regent's Park, a fact noted by Sir Edwin Lutyens, who remodeled it in 1910, adding a second floor with incongruously high roofs. Much of his work was removed after 1947 when the building became a Hall of Residence for Bedford College. When the college left in 1995, the unsightly additions it had itself made in the 1960s were removed and the Crown Estate offered a lease of the building for use as a private dwelling.

Terry drew up plans for the Bagri family that returned the building to Burton's design as much as possible, notably by reinstating over the colonnade the first-floor terrace, filled in by Lutyens, and by replacing correctly detailed columns, window architraves and pediments, and missing stringcourses. To help compensate for the space lost by opening up the terrace, he proposed adding a new two-storied wing containing a swimming pool in the basement, at a right angle to the original villa. Current thinking about the design of an addition to a historic building is either "make it 'frankly modern'" or "make it so bland as to pass unnoticed." Neither option is appealing to someone who believes in the continuing validity of the classical language. Moreover, Burton's work at Hanover Lodge is comparatively featureless, so Terry's solution was to provide a modest design—not in Burton's language but in a kind of Gibbsian Palladianism, making its distinction from Burton's work evident.

Planning consent was received for this work in 1996, but the client began to feel that since the addition would make the house L-shaped, an irregular form that is not in sympathy with the classical language of Burton, it would be more appropriate if, instead, the additions were made principally to the rear of the building, so that it would be symmetrical, as it originally was. With infinite adaptability, Terry thus prepared a new design with a wing added at the rear of the villa. This contains a large reception room with a centrally placed bow, echoing those in Decimus Burton's two nearby villas, the Holme and Nuffield Lodge. The huge entrance hall, inspired by Inigo Jones's at the Queen's House in Greenwich (1616–35), and by the Stone Hall at Houghton Hall in Norfolk (1734) by Colen Campbell, James Gibbs, and William Kent, is one of the most imposing and richly ornamented interiors of recent times. Full-scale, freehand drawings by Francis Terry for the decorative stonework and plasterwork introduce a vibrancy and sensitivity to plant forms and associated classical ornament on a scale unparalleled in modern British architecture.

This major house is a more demanding commission than Terry's previous six villas in Regent's Park for it is on a far larger scale, involves the retention of work by two previous architects, and has a much more ornate interior. It should be finished in 2007, bringing to completion eighteen years of work on these villas, and serving as the final example of seven possible ways in which the classical repertoire can now be employed.

113

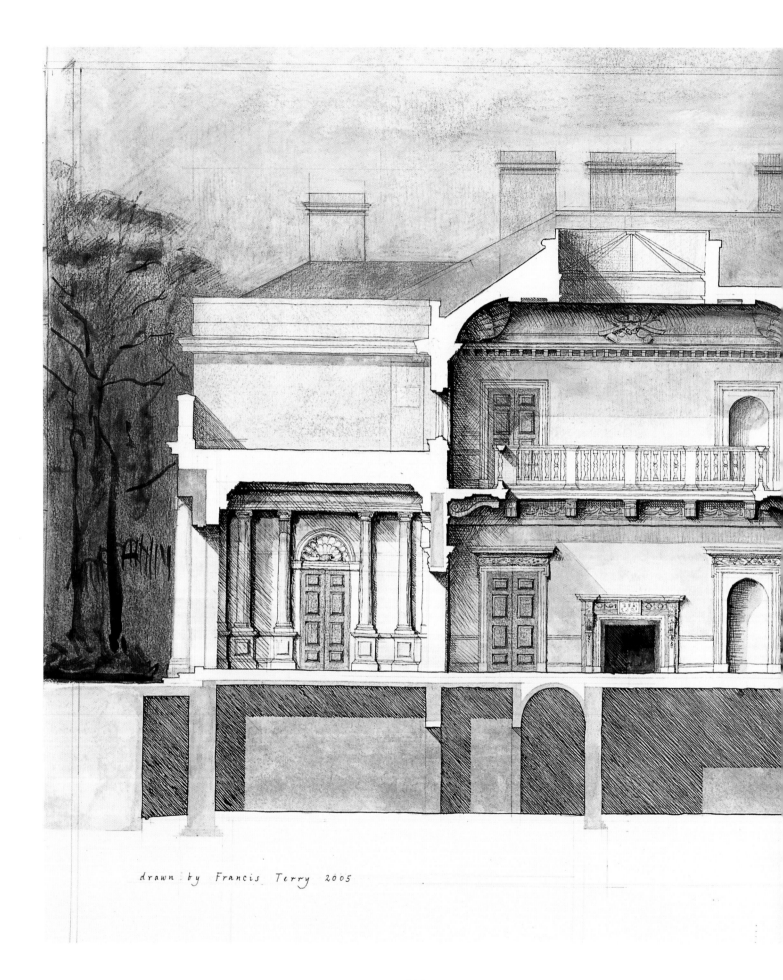

drawn by Francis Terry 2005

115

FULL SIZE FRONT ELEVATION OF IONIC CAPITAL

FULL SIZE PLAN OF IONIC CAPITAL

Francis Terry

FACING PAGE
Working drawing by Francis Terry for the Ionic capital at Hanover Lodge, inspired by the Erechtheion, Athens (421–405 BC). Exhibited at The Royal Academy Summer Exhibition 2004

TOP
Corinthian pilaster capital, inspired by the Temple of Castor and Pollux, Rome (ca. 1st century AD)

ABOVE
Full-size model of Ionic capital being made in the workshop

RIGHT
Working drawing by Francis Terry for cartouches in the cove of the central hall, Hanover Lodge. Exhibited at The Royal Academy Summer Exhibition 2004

117

House in Knightsbridge

This lavish commission, completed in 2000 for a Middle Eastern patron, involved gutting a large, late Victorian, terraced mansion, behind the façade of which Quinlan Terry had a free hand to create suites of new rooms on all the principal floors. The display of rich materials and ornament, frequently polished, is far more emphatic than would have been required by most English patrons. However, just as Terry is accustomed to adapting to local conditions, using local materials, building forms, and styles whenever possible, he is also able to respond imaginatively to the varying requirements of different patrons. On the first floor, a new entrance hall with a dining room to the left, leads into a large elevator lobby and a central hall, from which opens a semicircular cantilevered marble staircase. Behind this on the east is a two-storied court with an internal balcony, top-lit by a high lantern, and on the west a domed saloon. Finally, facing the garden at the rear is a large room for the children. The complicated spaces are tied together through the use of the orders and through a polychrome marble floor inspired by that in Longhena's Santa Maria della Salute in Venice (1630s).

FACING PAGE
Staircase in white statuary marble

In the dining room, the bold Doric order divided by arches as set out in Palladio's *I Quattro Libri* is carried around the walls in paneling of polished mahogany. The order runs at the same height into the central hall, where its material shifts to a white stucco. In all the principal interiors, the articulation of the classical orders lends itself to the incorporation of modern technology; for example, air-conditioning outlets are neatly concealed as metopes in the triglyph frieze in the dining room. The Ionic order is used for the children's room, which is paneled in softly toned, two-hundred-year-old antique pine woodwork brought from earlier buildings.

In the drawing room on the second floor, the order, now appropriately a rich Corinthian, follows exactly the arcaded Palladian articulation of the dining room, which is immediately below it. In both the columns and pilasters of the drawing room, Terry re-created the perfect, archetypal Corinthian capital, where the modeling and casting create pure space between the leaves, volutes, and abacus, thus clarifying their relation to the solid bell beneath. The complicated entablature of this room, enriched with bands of guilloche and bay-leaf moldings, is related to the design of the ornamental plasterwork of the ceiling, providing a scholarly and beautiful essay in the handling of the classical language from which many could learn. In the exquisite bathrooms on the floor above, one of which is lined with Algerian onyx, the row of marble basins provide a rippling Baroque line. Terry has found that relatively small yet complex interiors such as these—so full of marble fittings, bronze moldings, steps, and wall linings, many of which have to be demountable to provide access to plumbing—can take as much time to design as a whole reception room.

FOLLOWING PAGES
PAGE 118
Entrance hall

PAGE 119, TOP
Sectional drawing by Francis Terry of wall in entrance hall

PAGE 119, BOTTOM
Sectional drawing by Francis Terry of domed saloon

Craftsmanship everywhere is of dazzling quality, notably in the gilt-bronze door furniture made by the Schmidt firm in Paris, where the metalwork skills for which French craftsmen have been renowned since the seventeenth century have been uniquely retained. These solid but lavish fittings, of cast and repoussé workmanship, gleam against the polished mahogany doors that Terry designed in a manner inspired by those at Robert Adam's Kenwood House (1768). In a remarkable—and practical—sleight of hand, the doors of the children's room are mahogany on the outside leading to the saloon, and simpler pine on the inside.

The client was shown all designs for the interiors on which he commented fully, frequently calling for more enrichment. Indeed, what is likely to strike the visitor most is the astonishingly rich ornament in stuccowork, the most elaborate of its kind created in many

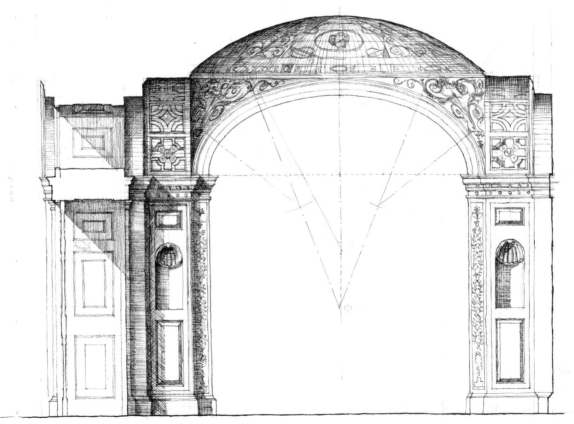

ABOVE LEFT
*Corinthian capital
in drawing room*

ABOVE RIGHT
*Wall panel in lift
lobby*

FACING PAGE
*Working drawing by
Francis Terry of wall
panel in lift lobby*

years. The client suggested that he would like the interior decoration to have something of the flavor of the celebrated Villa Madama in Rome, begun in 1518 from designs by Raphael as a re-creation of the ancient Roman villas described in the letters of the younger Pliny. By a happy coincidence, Terry had made measured drawings of the Villa Madama while he was a Rome Scholar at the British School at Rome. Though the domed ceilings in the saloon of his Knightsbridge house have features in common with Raphael's at the Villa Madama, the latter are on such an enormously larger scale that the Kensington work had to be completely rethought from scratch.

In the entrance hall, the joyous stuccowork panels, designed by Francis Terry, are of breathtaking loveliness and freshness. Both sides of the room are divided into three panels, framed by running patterns of simple foliage. The overall decoration is repeated on each side with two triumphal garlands in the outer panels flanking a central roundel based on Raphael's celebrated fresco *The Triumph of Galatea* in the Villa Farnesina in Rome (1509–19), built by Baldassarre Peruzzi. The love story of Galatea, a Nereid or sea nymph, and Acis, son of Pan, has been a familiar theme since the time of the wall paintings in Pompeii. But what makes Francis Terry's response to Raphael's representation of the nymph particularly inventive is his free adaptation of Raphael's huge rectangular painting in fresco as a circular plaster relief, only six inches across. Terry concentrates on the central image of Galatea riding a sea chariot in the form of a shell, drawn by dolphins and surrounded by other Nereids and Tritons. He responds to the key elements of Raphael's scene through a dif-

Maximum projection of fruit in swag to be 35 m.m.

Maximum projection of plaster work in figures to be 35 m.m.

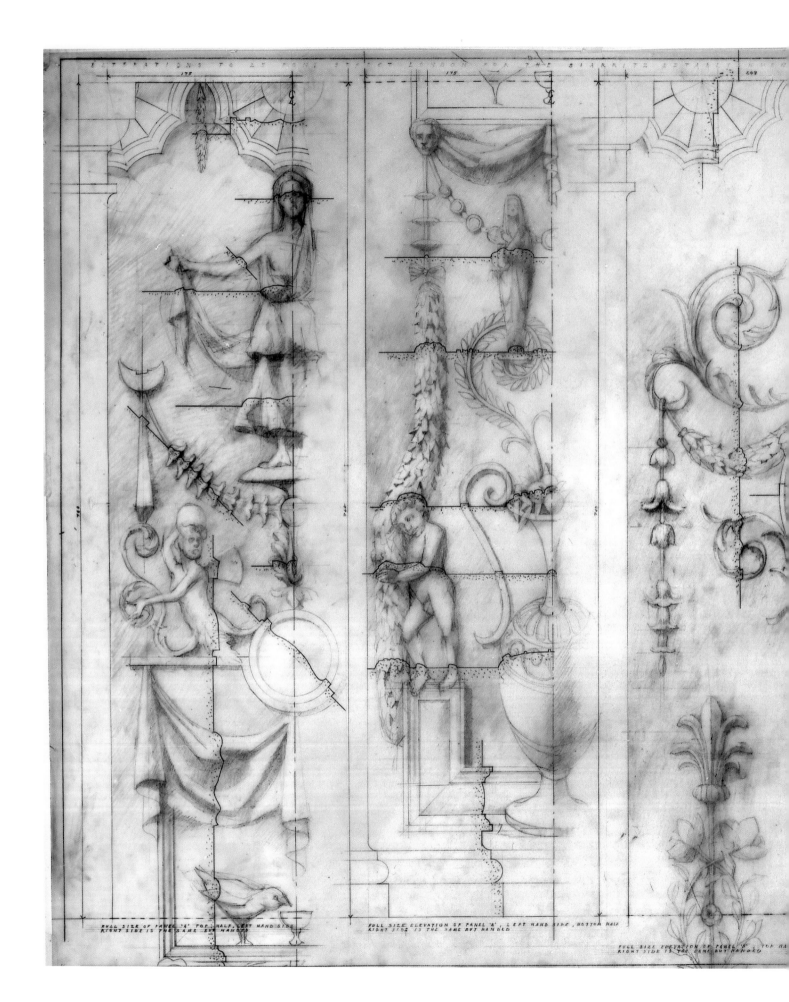

FULL SIZE OF PANEL 'A' TOP HALF, LEFT HAND SIDE
RIGHT SIDE IS THE SAME BUT HANDED

FULL SIZE ELEVATION OF PANEL 'A', LEFT HAND SIDE, BOTTOM HALF
RIGHT SIDE IS THE SAME BUT HANDED

FULL SIZE ELEVATION OF PANEL 'B' TOP HALF
RIGHT SIDE IS THE SAME BUT HANDED

SMITH AND TERRY ARCHITECTS
OLD CHANGING WITH STREET, LONDON
CHICHESTER 10364   4TH APRIL 1996
1109/5/7
FULL SIZE AND 1:3 SCALE ELEVATIONS
OF PLASTER PANELS IN HALL
READ IN CONJUNCTION WITH 1109/5/6
1109/5/2

NO SIDE

1:3 ELEVATION OF PANEL 'A'

FULL SIZE ELEVATION OF PANEL 'B'. BOTTOM HALF, LEFT HAND SIDE
RIGHT SIDE IS THE SAME BUT HANDED

1:3 ELEVATION OF PANEL 'B'

Working drawings by Francis Terry of wall decoration to entrance hall

125

ferent size and medium, and achieves great depth and vigor. His own experience as an artist and portrait painter in London evidently stands him in good stead for the difficult demands of commissions of this kind.

Francis Terry spent six months making detailed designs, which he presented in full-size drawings, for the plasterwork of this house. He explained that, "It is quite a different thing from the process of an architectural drawing. It is one of the few forms of drawing where you are using section, lines, and shading to give a three-dimensional effect all at once. The rigor

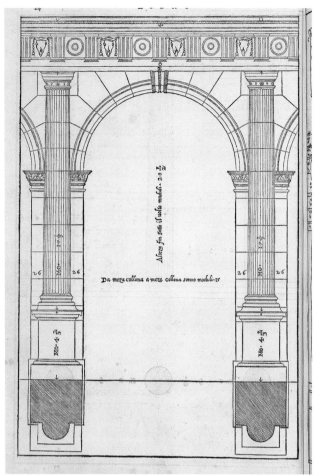

of these drawings is important, too; every pencil mark is significant. The shading is practical and not merely aesthetic." In preparation, he went to study the Villa Madama and Syon House in Middlesex, where Robert Adam's Long Gallery of the 1760s is a novel and vast expanse of subtle plasterwork. From this interior, Terry borrowed something of the varied articulation, as well as the repeated neo-antique tripods for his central panels, though he transformed the motif into the appearance of a lantern. The iconography of Terry's panels is loosely based on images of triumph, plenty, and the celebration of home, while the soffits of the arches contain miniature niches with tiny busts of Roman emperors and gods, as at the Villa Madama. A striking panel by the entry to the dining room shows a pair of satyrs with animated expressions emerging from scrollwork, bearing cornucopia.

Cast in fibrous plaster in the late-eighteenth-century manner of Robert Adam, the reliefs in this area have been left off-white and polished in situ, their color and delicacy suggesting marble and thus preparing the visitor for the new cantilevered staircase, which, remarkably, is of Carrara marble. Following custom, the element of color increases as one moves from the entrance hall. The stucco in the saloon has a blue and gold coloring, with roundels in the ceiling representing the seasons, derived from Michelangelesque examples. The painting and gilding is the work of Campbell Smith, of London.

Many people had a hand in Francis Terry's elaborate reliefwork at the Knightsbridge House. Every detail was hand-modeled in clay into a form from which a team of eight modelers, employed by Roger Bannister in the firm of Thomas and Wilson of Fulham, could take a rubber mold. The project was managed on-site by Hugh Barrell, a long-standing partner in the firm of Erith and Terry.

Tarrant Place

Saint Marylebone

Tarrant Place (unillustrated) is a residential development of mews houses reached through an archway and built in 1989 of London stock brick to echo the nearby Regency houses and the neoclassical church of Saint Mary in Wyndham Place (1821–23), by Sir Robert Smirke.

Chester House

Belgravia

Tarrant Place prepared the way for another subtle piece of urban planning by Terry, which enabled a substantial new building to be inserted into a well-known conservation area just south of Belgrave Square, laid out beginning in 1826 from designs by George Basevi. The site backs on to Belgrave Mews South, which has, of course, a far more modest character than Upper Belgrave Street. Thus, at the back of the site, the new building has a simple brick front of three stories plus a roof, closing the views eastward along the mews. To Belgrave Place, by contrast, it presents a five-bay stuccoed front with a Greek Doric porch, a handsome façade that also acts as a focal point in views west along Chester Street. Terry has thus provided a clever way of improving the frequently jerky street line of Belgravia with a new house that looks as though it has always been there and does not compromise the cottagey nature of the mews behind it.

RIGHT
Previous buildings on the site, 1995

FACING PAGE
New entrance front to Upper Belgrave Street

State Rooms at 10 Downing Street

London

In 1988, Terry received a commission to work at what is probably the most famous address in England, the historic home of the British prime ministers. Here and at the adjacent buildings, nos. 11 and 12, Raymond Erith had worked extensively for the Ministry of Public Buildings and Works, during the time of Harold Macmillan, from 1959 to 1963, when the houses were found to be in poor structural condition. When this work was going forward, Quinlan Terry arrived in Erith's office, playing a small part in its completion. Twenty-five years later, Margaret Thatcher sought enhancement of the three interlocking state drawing rooms at no. 10. Though dating from the 1730s, probably by William Kent, the rooms had been altered over the years and, more importantly, seem never to have been provided with the decorative ceilings, overmantels, and overdoors that would normally have matched the fine chimneypieces in carved marble. Terry carried out the difficult task of making good these deficiencies, beginning in 1988 with the Yellow (or Pillared) Room at the northeast corner, followed between 1989 and 1990 by the Green Room in the center, and the White Room at the northwest corner. Since he was providing missing architectural and decorative features, he could not copy existing details but instead added elements in harmony with them. In his three new overmantels, he incorporated the three orders: Doric in the Green Room, Corinthian in the White Room, and Ionic in the Yellow Room.

The Yellow Room had been enlarged to the south in the 1780s with a simple neoclassical screen of two Ionic columns below a plain ceiling, which it was inappropriate to enrich, though Terry added an Ionic overmantel to the chimneypiece. Since the two doors in the south wall were found to be too low for the room, he was asked to provide filigree panels over them. In his search for a model, he sent his son, Francis, to Rome for a few days in June of 1990 to measure the panels of the Ara Pacis Augustae (13–9 B.C.), famous for the delicate naturalism of its scrollwork. In the Green and White Rooms, he added richly carved overdoors and also new decorative ceilings, enriched with ornamental plasterwork that incorporated the national flowers: rose, shamrock, daffodil, and thistle. In the Green Room, he created a bold ceiling in the style of Inigo Jones, while in the carved frieze of the room's new overdoor he incorporated a figure of a thatcher at work, appropriate to the then prime minister.

All this work had to conform to modern "listed building" requirements, so all of Terry's contributions have been recorded and can be "demounted" if tastes change. They have been ignored in the architectural press and have scarcely been illustrated until now.

ABOVE
*Drawing by Francis Terry
of ornament on the Ara
Pacis Augustae, Rome
(13–9 BC)*

RIGHT
*Yellow Room, plaster
panel above doors*

ABOVE
White Room, doorcase

RIGHT
*White Room, stucco
detail to ceiling*

FOLLOWING PAGES
*Green Room with new
plaster ceiling, door surrounds, and Palladian
Doric overmantel with
the Royal Coat of Arms*

CHAPTER 3

Country Houses

Country houses have formed the greater part of Quinlan Terry's practice, though it was far from clear that there would be such a rejuvenation in this building type when he began working with Raymond Erith on his first major house, King's Walden Bury (see below), in 1969. Private building on this scale was then largely prohibited by the penal level of taxation.

Column, West Green House

Hampshire

An appropriate introduction to this chapter is provided by one of Terry's many entertaining garden buildings at West Green House in Hampshire for Lord McAlpine. This great, rusticated Doric column was built in 1976 as an eye-catcher to be seen from the main house. Echoing Trajan's Column in Rome (A.D. 106–13), its Portland-stone pedestal bears a Latin inscription devised by Terry that reads, "This monument was erected at great expense with money which would sooner or later have been taken away by the tax-collectors." This commemorates the high level of taxation in the mid-1970s, the considerable lowering of which in the late 1980s did much to enable Terry's career as a country-house architect to flourish.

King's Walden Bury

Hertfordshire

The next four projects represent a group of four country houses in red brick. Begun in 1969, King's Walden Bury in Hertfordshire, for Sir Thomas Pilkington, Bart., was the last and largest of Raymond Erith's country houses, and Terry was closely involved in its design. In fact, Erith felt that there was a difficulty in using red brick in the country, where it can stand out in vivid contrast to the softer colors and tones of farmland, woods, and skies. Though this is especially true when the brick is new, it will mellow agreeably with time, but it is still sometimes more appropriate for street architecture than for very large country houses.

Latin inscription on pedestal

140

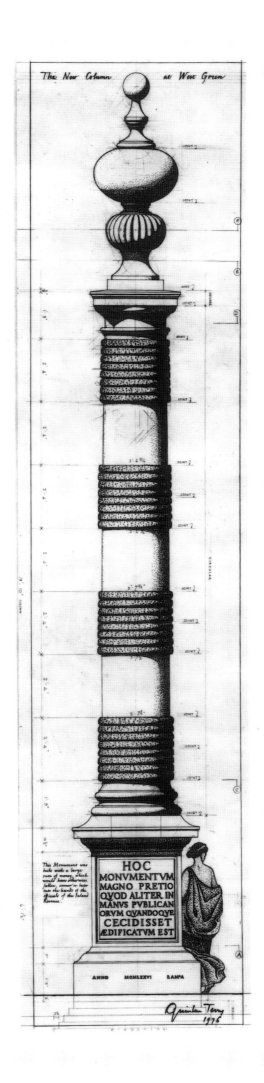

The New Column   at West Green

HOC
MONVMENTVM
MAGNO PRETIO
QVOD ALITER IN
MANVS PVBLICAN
ORVM QVANDOQVE
CECIDISSET
ÆDIFICATVM EST

ANNO   MCMLXXVI   RAM&A

Quinlan Terry
1976

Drawing by Quinlan Terry

FOLLOWING PAGES
*King's Walden Bury,
Hertfordshire, South front*

The Ionic Order. (half inch scale)

By strictly orthodox proportional standards, this column is short, the entablature is large, the cornice is very large.
Alberti says .... 'the most expert artists among the ancients were of the opinion that an edifice was like an animal, so that
in the formation of it we ought to imitate nature'. He then gives an example to illustrate the difference in the parts or men

ABOVE AND FACING PAGE
Drawings by Quinlan Terry
for details of Ionic order

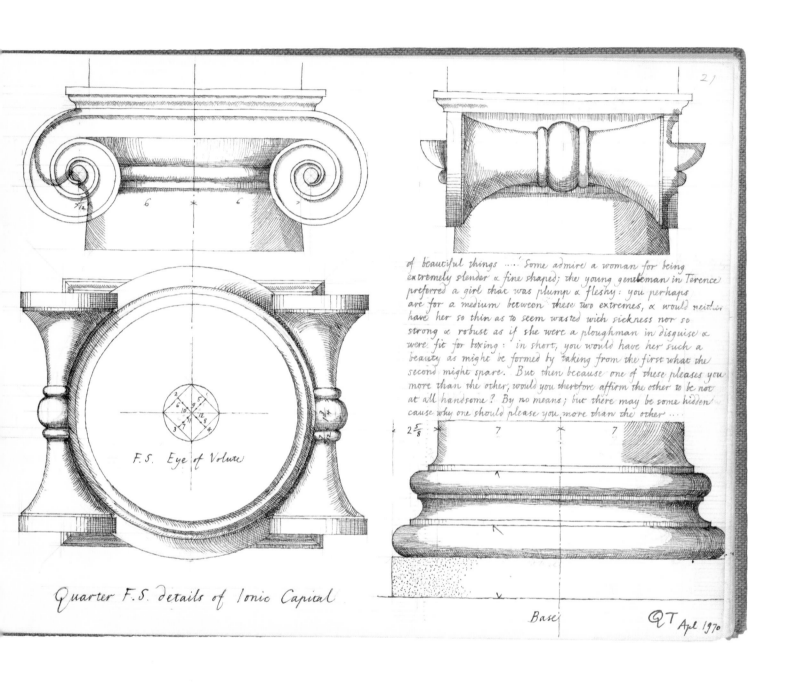

of beautiful things ..... Some admire a woman for being extremely slender & fine shaped; the young gentleman in Terence preferred a girl that was plump & fleshy: you perhaps are for a medium between these two extremes, & would neither have her so thin as to seem wasted with sickness nor so strong & robust as if she were a ploughman in disguise & were fit for boxing: in short, you would have her such a beauty as might be formed by taking from the first what the second might spare. But then because one of these pleases you more than the other, would you therefore affirm the other to be not at all handsome? By no means; but there may be some hidden cause why one should please you more than the other .....

2 5/8   7   7

F.S. Eye of Volute

Quarter F.S. details of Ionic Capital

Base

QT Apl 1970

145

Merks Hall

Essex

Surmounting a steep hill, Merks Hall (1984–86) represents an exceptionally successful use of the local materials of Essex—notably red brick, stucco, and slate—for a house of comparatively modest size. It was built for Richard Wallis on the site of an ugly modern house erected in 1961. An exuberant building, Terry's replacement for this commands distant views from the domed belvedere that crowns its balustraded flat, a favorite form of Terry's, derived from seventeenth-century houses such as the demolished Coleshill House in Berkshire (1660). One first sees its rich entrance front diagonally from the entrance piers that are placed in the corner of the unusual octagonal forecourt, defined by brick walls and iron railings. Picturesquely approached from an angle, this façade features Baroque details, such as windows set in deep, canted reveals, recalling the perspectival devices adopted by Borromini at the seventeenth-century Palazzo Barberini in Rome.

RIGHT
Entrance front

FACING PAGE
South and east fronts

Great Canfield

Essex

Great Canfield in Essex (2001–3) is yet another commission in Quinlan Terry's career that was the subject of much controversy and involved a successful planning appeal, setting an influential precedent for future developments. Planning consent is not normally granted for new country houses on agricultural land, but John Gummer, during his period as Secretary of State for the Environment, was able to arrange for the insertion of a clause known as PPG7 into the planning legislation, which allowed for exceptions to this rule when it could be shown that the proposed building was of outstanding quality. Terry's house at Great Canfield was the first new country house for which permission was granted under the PPG7 arrangement.

Quinlan Terry was approached in September 1997 by Mr. and Mrs. Philip Seers to replace a poorly detailed barn conversion at Great Canfield with a substantial new country house. Having lived for many years on the border of Suffolk and Essex, Terry felt that what was required at Great Canfield was something based on a familiar type of Essex country house.

Despite the obvious merits of this design, Uttlesfield District Council announced in January 2000 that they intended to refuse the application. Their grounds for rejection of the design included its supposed failure to "take proper account of the defining characteristics of the local area, including local and regional building traditions and materials." A planning appeal was therefore held in May 2000, at which a representative of the Council for the Preservation of Rural Essex made clear his distaste for country-house owners and for present-day traditional architecture, even deploring the planning consent that had been granted for Terry's Merks Hall (see p. 146), just four miles away from Great Canfield. Condemning Terry's design for Great Canfield as "a pastiche in the sense that it is a copy of a style of another age," he ludicrously complained that this solid enduring building did not "have something that my children would call the 'Wow!' factor." A similarly hostile letter was received from another member of the Council for the Preservation of Rural Essex, who wrote, "The application is for a house in a modern pastiche of 'Queen Anne' style. As such it neither draws on local building traditions, nor does it contribute a twentieth-century element to the 'Country House tradition.'"

It seems that we still have not reached the end of the instinctive use of the word "pastiche" to condemn all modern traditional architecture, or the belief that the architect has a near moral obligation to express "the spirit of the age." In the course of his own lengthy evidence at the inquiry, Terry enjoyed pointing out that it was assumed that any outstanding buildings permitted by the PPG7 exemption would last for hundreds of years. Though he expected his own buildings to survive for such a period, the Modernist buildings expressing "the spirit of their age," which are admired by opponents of his own work, would scarcely last a few decades because of their rejection of traditional materials and construction in favor of thin walls, flat roofs, steel, glass, aluminium, exposed reinforced concrete, and plastics, all of which have a very high coefficient of thermal expansion. They are therefore subject to water penetration at expansion joints, causing the structure to deteriorate quickly.

The inspector appointed to adjudicate at the inquiry by the Secretary of State for the Environment, Transport, and the Regions, announced in July 2000 that his appeal decision was in favor of Terry's design. Though this judgment effectively dismissed as unacceptable the

FACING PAGE
*North entrance front,
Great Canfield,
Essex, 2001–3*

empty rhetoric by which traditional design is rejected as "pastiche," the battle for the abandonment of this word, which acts as an obstacle to intelligent assessment, is still far from won.

Indeed, in 2004, the Labour government replaced PPG7 with PPS7, which appeared to have a pro-Modernist slant, requiring forms described as "innovative" and of "cutting edge" character. As a result, planning legislators have recently refused Terry's design for a new house in Ravenstonedale, Cumbria, on the site of an old one that was demolished in the 1950s. The inspector stated that, "Historically inspired designs would not, in my view, generally meet that requirement [of PPS7]." This is despite the fact that, following questioning after the announcement of PPS7, the government stated that it had no "intention to impose or dictate a particular style preference." However, it is widely feared that it has come worryingly close to doing so, and the Ravenstonedale case shows, in Terry's words, "how we still have to fight every step of the way against almost overwhelming odds, entrenched opposition, and willful ignorance of our Classical heritage." At the same time, there is no reason why buildings such as Terry's Corinthian Villa in Regent's Park (see p. 86), with its double-curved façade, should not be hailed as "innovative" with a "cutting edge" character. Indeed, Francis Terry made this claim in a letter published in *Country Life* at the time of the PPS7 controversy in 2004.

Terry's final revised designs for the Great Canfield house were made in the spring of 2001, and construction was completed in 2003. A large house, eleven bays long and only three bays deep (though these bays are admittedly very broad), it is two stories high, plus cellar and attics in the hipped roof. There are pediments over the three central bays on the north entrance front and on the south garden front, where the first floor is enlivened with an applied order of Doric pilasters in stone. Otherwise, despite its considerable size, this is simply a decent, undemonstrative building without much display, which relies on the quality of its brickwork and the rhythm of the sash windows for its timeless appeal.

Juniper Hill

Buckinghamshire

With little stone of good quality, Buckinghamshire is a county where red brick began to appear as early as the 1440s, at Eton College. It continued to be widely used for buildings of high social standing, notably for a series of exuberant country houses of the seventeenth and eighteenth centuries, including Hall Barn, Denham Place, and Chicheley. With its freestanding, giant portico, Juniper Hill, built for Warren Hardy on the site of a dull Edwardian house, captures something of the eye-catching, metropolitan opulence of such houses, as well as that of the houses of colonial America. This is in marked contrast to Terry's house at Great Canfield (see p. 148), with its quieter flavor of rural Essex.

Designed between 1998 and 1999, Juniper Hill was completed in 2000, a date that is handsomely recorded in Roman numerals, MM, on the frieze of its two pediments. It is a lively coloristic composition, in which red brick contrasts cheerfully with stone-colored stucco. The two principal elevations have the 2-3-2 bay disposition of the more generous English Palladian villas, but the house unusually indulges the luxury of freestanding porticoes on both the north entrance front and south garden front. There are rubbed and gauged red brick arches over the windows, the angle quoins are rendered, and the eaves are timber. In the two great porticoes, the columns, pilasters, massive entablatures, and pediments are of reconstructed stone. The columns are built up from a series of disks that are then rendered, while the inner wall of the porticoes are also rendered to represent stone.

RIGHT
Entrance front with freestanding Ionic portico and Venetian windows to wings

FACING PAGE
Detail of pediment

Waverton House

Gloucestershire

We now pass to a group of ten major houses, largely built of stone. An early work by Quinlan Terry in this material is Waverton House in Gloucestershire (1978–80), built for Jocelyn Hambro. This house is of a Palladian format but gains a vernacular flavor through its walls of coursed rubble with ashlar dressings, below a hipped roof of local Cotswold stone slates. The handsome Ionic door surround on the entrance front employs Sanmicheli's use of an abacus projecting proud of the echinus, which he based on Roman originals in Verona. Nicholas Kingsley and Michael Hall have written of Waverton in volume three of *The Country Houses of Gloucestershire, 1830–2000* (2001): "A grave essay in a revived Classical style, and takes itself a good deal more seriously a country house than any such building erected in the county since the Second World War. So too was Court Farm Bibury, also designed by Terry . . . and equally serious, though a slightly more engaging house."

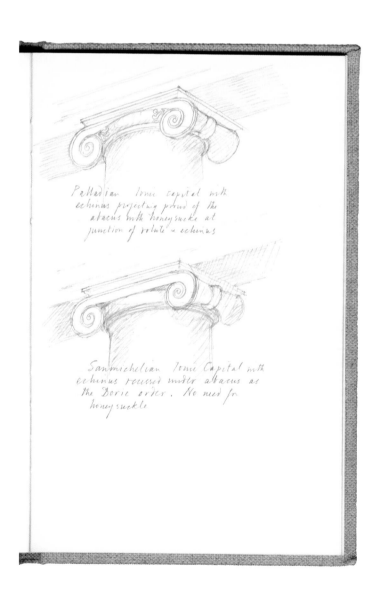

RIGHT
Drawings by Quinlan Terry of Ionic capitals after Palladio and Sanmicheli

FACING PAGE
Entrance door with Sanmichelian Ionic capitals in Doulting stone

FOLLOWING PAGES
Entrance front

PAGES 154–155
Garden front

Bibury Court and Summer House

Gloucestershire

BELOW
Entrance front

FACING PAGE
Detail of front door with Palladian Doric surround with swan-neck pediment in Clipsham stone. The fanlight incorporates the initials C and J, for the owners, a husband and wife

FOLLOWING PAGES
Garden front

Terry followed Waverton House (see p. 152) with Bibury Court (1986–88), in the same county, on the edge of the Cotswold village of Bibury, which William Morris "discovered" and called the most beautiful village in England. Though this is therefore a very sensitive setting, the new house, for John Heynes, does not stand out like a sore thumb: built of Cotswold stone throughout and with an elongated plan suggested by the nature of the site, it seems to have been there forever. Nonetheless, with the five widely spaced bays of its entrance front below a generous hipped roof, it displays the confident weightiness of Sir Edwin Lutyens, though the frontispiece on its seven-bay garden front is enlivened with early Renaissance details borrowed from Robert Smythson (1535–1614).

Not the least enchanting part of Bibury Court is the summer house overlooking the pool. With rounded ends below a hipped tiled roof, its walls are of coursed rubble fronted with a miniature Tuscan portico in ashlar. It is a gem and, like the main house, has something of the magic of Lutyens.

FACING PAGE
Central bay of garden front

ABOVE
*Drawing by Quinlan Terry
for central bay of garden
front*

LEFT
Summer house

Fort Brecqhou

Channel Islands

The largest house built in Britain for at least two centuries, Fort Brecqhou was commissioned in 1993 by Sir David and Sir Frederick Barclay, who had known the site, a tiny island between Guernsey and Sark, for thirty-five years. It required not only wealth but heroic imagination and boundless courage to conceive and carry into execution a granite-built castle on this vast scale that would grow out of and not dominate its rocky, romantic setting, storm-battered and seagirt. With his extensive experience of designing large country houses, Quinlan Terry was uniquely qualified to respond to this commission. He is, moreover, dedicated to the concept of an architecture so rooted in construction and solid materials as to achieve a permanence that is impervious to wind and water, especially necessary on such an exposed site.

FACING PAGE
Central bays of entrance front

FOLLOWING PAGES
North and west fronts

Far from being a prima donna architect, Terry sees his first duty not as self-expression but rather as service to his client. He was thus the ideal architect for patrons who, from the start, had a clear idea of the general form their house should take. In addition, Terry is at home with Gothic design, admiring and frequently sketching the combination of Gothic and classical details in English medieval parish churches. He was given at the start a sketch plan by David Barclay of his own ideas for a habitable castle or fort: a substantial structure built around four sides of a courtyard. Both David and Frederick Barclay wanted a castellated Gothic-style building, with circular turrets at the four corners. The brothers admired Terry's Gothick Villa in Regent's Park (see p. 80), which, though modest in comparison with Brecqhou, they wished him to take as a preliminary model. Terry observes that, "The design was, of course, developed in a number of ways, but the general principles remain exactly as were made clear to me at our first meeting."

The building hugs the rock on which it is built, spreading horizontally rather than vertically, so that it seems to be a timeless, ancient structure that was domesticated in the seventeenth century, most windows being not Gothic but rectangular or round-headed. Appearing naturally related to the modest island in which it is rooted, its presence is not immediately apparent to the visitor who arrives at the new harbor and walks up the winding drive to the house. Like the unfolding movements in some great nineteenth-century symphony, Fort Brecqhou is a place that reveals its secrets and grandeur slowly. Upon arrival, its scale is not at first obvious because the entrance front, being on high ground, is the lowest of the four façades. Walking around the house, which takes some time, the visitor gradually appreciates that not only is each façade not a symmetrical composition in itself, but that all four façades are quite different from each other.

As David Barclay wished, Fort Brecqhou has a quadrangular plan taking the form of a giant square built around an arcaded courtyard, initially intended to be left open to the sky but now glazed over. It sits on a piece of land that slopes downward to the north, so that the south entrance front has two stories, while the north seafront has four. Behind the south entrance front, which is a greatly expanded version of Terry's Gothick Villa in Regent's Park, is a centrally placed, circular stair hall, flanked by a two-storied dining room on the left and a drawing room on the right. The north front is remarkable as it consists of four houses for members of the clients' family; this familial concept is paralleled in many of Palladio's villas and palaces. The façade of the house is unified, however, and does not betray the internal divi-

sions. In the center of the façade is a large, carved cartouche with the owners' arms and motto, below which a curved, double staircase leads down from a balustraded terrace to the lawn.

The immaculately laid blocks of granite at Fort Brecqhou, gleaming and sparkling, are alive with subtly varying tints and surface textures. The walls are a bush-hammered, roughly textured, honey-colored granite called Silvestre Moreno, from northwest Spain. This contrasts with the fine, rubbed Crème Champagne, a cold, blue gray Spanish granite, used for the moldings around the windows, doors, plinths, and stringcourses. The potentially daunt-

Detail of north front

FOLLOWING PAGES
*East and north fronts
from the sea*

ing mass of building is offset by the animation of the roofscape, its battlemented parapets surmounted by towers, cupolas, flagpoles, and giant twisted chimneys inspired by those invented during the reign of Henry VIII (1491–1597), which are unique to English architecture. The majority of these exuberantly carved and clustered brick chimneys are to be found in East Anglia, home to Quinlan Terry, as, for example, at Layer Marney Hall (ca. 1520) and the late-fifteenth-century Saint Osyth's Priory in Essex, and at East Barsham Manor in Norfolk (ca. 1520).

At any castle, visitors look forward to emerging from dark and winding staircases on to a dramatic roofscape where they will walk along perilous platforms behind crenellated parapets, gazing out on a wild world of sky and sea, their lungs expanding in the strong winds. These visitors are not disappointed at Brecqhou, where everything works, everything is what it seems: the round towers contain real spiral staircases, the astonishingly sculptural chimneys are the exits of real, wood-burning fires, and an entire circuit can be made of the castle roofs, much of it on neat, duckboard floors of teak, followed by an ascent of the bartizan on the seafront to the highest point of all—the tower at the northwest angle. The roofscape is enlivened by golden balls that cap the roofs over the cupola and the bartizan.

The only twentieth-century comparison with Fort Brecqhou is Sir Edwin Lutyens's Castle Drogo in Devon (1910–30), a large and romantic building beautifully related to its site. However, only a fraction of Lutyens's original design was executed and this has suffered considerably from water penetration. In contrast, Fort Brecqhou was completed in little over two and a half years, beginning in January 1994 and ending in the late summer of 1996. The extraordinary speed of construction was partly due to the decision to build the inner, concrete blockwork of the walls up to the full height of the building before applying the outer solid wall of granite blocks. It is therefore a massive cavity wall construction, eminently suitable to its exposed position.

168

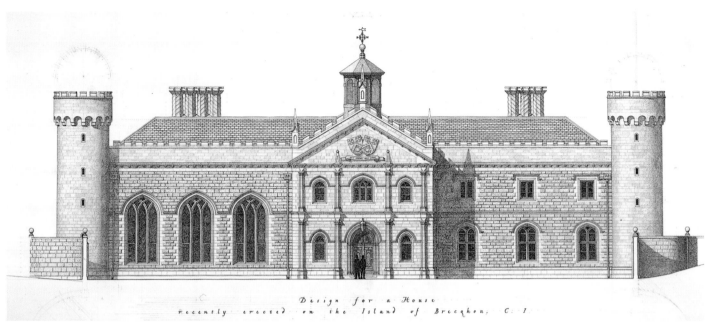

Drawing by George Saumarez Smith of south entrance front

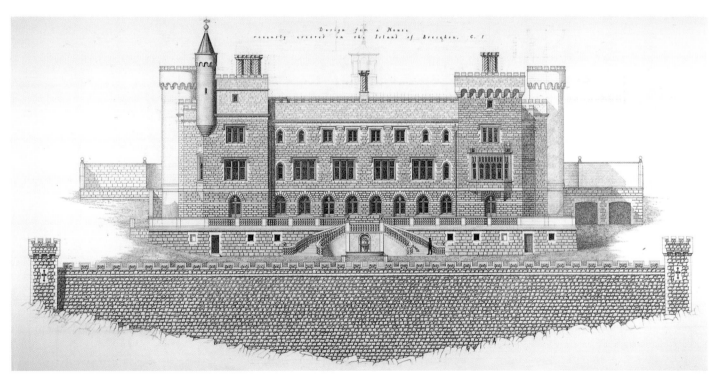

Drawing by George Saumarez Smith of seafront, exhibited at the Royal Academy Summer Exhibition, 1998

Lodge Cottage and Gates, Foliejon Park

Berkshire

FACING PAGE
Urns on lodge cottage

FOLLOWING PAGES
Lodge cottages and gates

In 1996, Quinlan Terry designed one of the most spectacular modern lodges and gateways of any English country house. It was a challenging commission for it was generated by the patron's wish to incorporate two pairs of nineteenth-century ironwork gates of sumptuous design that he had acquired. The appropriately theatrical setting that Terry devised for them featured an unusually placed lodge cottage, centrally located between two huge gateways that incorporated the owner's ironwork gates. The cottage, with walls of Leicester stock brick, rendered in imitation of stone, is modest in scale but is ambitiously adorned with a Venetian window with a pediment above, containing a bull's-eye window in the tympanum. There are also ball finials, two at the corners and one at the apex. The four monumental piers of the two gateways bear huge, elaborately carved urns, eight feet high, while Terry continued the feel of the nineteenth-century ironwork gates in the form of lower railings that create quadrants sweeping forward in an open, walled piazza.

Pin Oak

Versailles, Kentucky

The first of Terry's American houses, Pin Oak at Versailles, Kentucky, was built between 1986 and 1988 as the center of a stud farm. Constructed of the local golden brown Minnesota Kasota stone with Indiana limestone dressings of a lighter hue, it is a development from Terry's Newfield house in Yorkshire (1979–81), though with an additional story. Echoing Roger Morris's Marble Hill (1724–29), it is grander because the principal rooms are raised up to the second floor, forming a piano nobile above a rusticated basement. Visitors approach the giant entrance portico of four engaged Composite columns via an imposing double staircase. For a comparatively modest house, the plan is inventive, featuring a handsome T-shaped entrance hall with a centrally placed T-plan staircase in the cross bar.

RIGHT
Drawing by Quinlan Terry of design for garden front

FACING PAGE
Entrance front

FOLLOWING PAGES
Distant view

Latourette Farm

Somerset County, New Jersey

Built between 2002 and 2005, this singularly chaste Palladian villa is notable for its curved wings of the type proposed by Palladio for several villas, though he was only able to execute them at the Villa Badoer. They were probably inspired by Palladio's study of the hemicycles of the emperor Trajan's early-second-century forum in Rome, for he based much of his domestic architecture on the public buildings of that ancient city. Latourette Farm was commissioned by a patron with a deep knowledge of both Palladio's architecture and its influence in eighteenth-century America, notably on houses in Virginia and Maryland. It thus takes its place in the history of American architecture, where houses with quadrant wings became popular, first at Mount Airy in Richmond County, Virginia (1758–62), which was inspired by plates in James Gibbs's *Book of Architecture* (1728; 2nd ed., 1739).

Latourette Farm, a two-storied villa with cellars, has a Palladian 1-3-1 bay composition with a roof rising to a central balustraded flat. Its roof is lead, which has become unfamiliar in America where lead-covered copper or zinc is generally used, though this has a much shorter life than lead. Of the two, one-storied, quadrant wings flanking the north entrance front, that on the left contains garages approached through arched openings. Despite the lively interest provided by these wings, the detailing is simple and plain with much use made across the entrance front of the continued impost molding, the block between the capital, and the springing of an arch. The curved wings contain five windows on the rear or garden front, and three on the entrance front, difficult to set out and expensive to construct, for curved features in architecture traditionally cost twice that of straight ones.

RIGHT
Plan of Mount Airy, Richmond County, Virginia (1758–62)

FACING PAGE
Entrance front

FOLLOWING PAGES
Garden front, showing quadrant wings

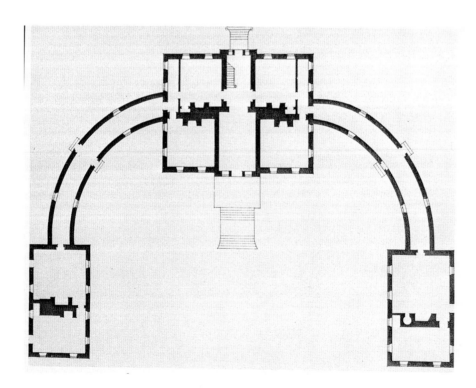

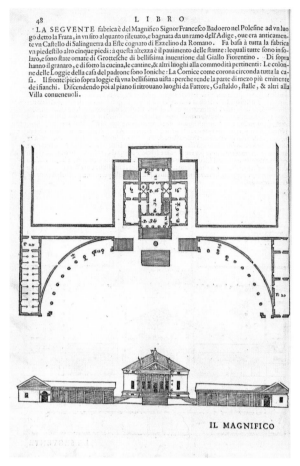

Villa Badoer (1554–63), plan and elevation, from Palladio, I Quattro Libri (1570)

Interior of quadrant wing, Latourette Farm

One of the remarkable aspects of Latourette Farm is the enormous consideration given to the choice of building material. Samples of several different stones were erected on site: Ketton, widely used in Cambridge since the seventeenth century; Clipsham, used today in Oxford as a replacement for Headington stone; Chilmark, used for Salisbury Cathedral, Wilton House, and Terry's Ferne Park (see p. 240); Indiana limestone, used extensively by McKim, Mead and White in New York; and Moleanos and Aria, from Spain. When Ketton was found to be the most attractive, it was shipped out to New Jersey from the Northamptonshire quarries. Particularly striking is the exceptionally tall entrance doorway, its round arch flanked by Ionic columns supporting a rich entablature.

The main house at Latourette contains an entrance hall with a breathtaking T-plan staircase of white marble. The single central flight divides into two cantilevered arms to the left and right, which then return to the landing in a further two flights. On one side of the central axis provided by this staircase hall are the dining room and kitchen, and on the other, the library and sitting room. It is notable that, to conform with modern living patterns, the large kitchen is the same size as the sitting room.

The local architect, Tom Bishop, and the landscape architect, Jacques Wirtz, made valuable contributions to the construction of Latourette.

Lunkewitz House

Frankfurt

Lunkewitz House (1991–93), the mansion Terry built near Frankfurt for a German client, was a turning point in the rehabilitation of the language of Classicism, which, as was mentioned in regard to Terry's office building in the Grosse Präsidentenstrasse in Berlin (see p. 44), had been outlawed in Germany after the World War II because of its supposed association with Nazism. This was absurd because, of course, classicism has been adopted under regimes of every political persuasion, from the ancient world to the present day. Terry's patron was the developer and publisher Bernd Lunkewitz, a man with a passionate devotion to the cause of new classical architecture in Germany. In the disastrous postwar rebuilding of bomb-damaged Frankfurt, a blinkered ideology prevented the creation of the great neoclassical monuments that formerly made it one of the most gracious cities in Germany. Lunkewitz House is a first step on a more architecturally harmonious path.

On an important site on the edge of a forest on the outskirts of Frankfurt, Lunkewitz House is a large two-story mansion of stucco and local sandstone, rising from a rusticated basement to a slate roof. It has casement windows rather than English sashes. Though it is basically a Palladian villa, the square moldings of its entablatures and stringcourses, and, especially, the tetrastyle Grecian portico of freestanding Erechtheion Ionic columns, make reference to the language of Karl Friedrich Schinkel and his contemporaries. At the same time, its crowning balustrade, which Schinkel would not have chosen, confers on it an English flavor welcomed by its patron. The garden front, however, has more of the flavor of Schinkel, in particular his elegantly Grecian Schloss Glienicke (1824–32) at Berlin-Glienicke. The one storied flanking wings were originally designed to be four bays only.

BELOW
Drawing by Les Edwards of entrance front

FACING PAGE
Entrance front as executed

FOLLOWING PAGES
Garden front

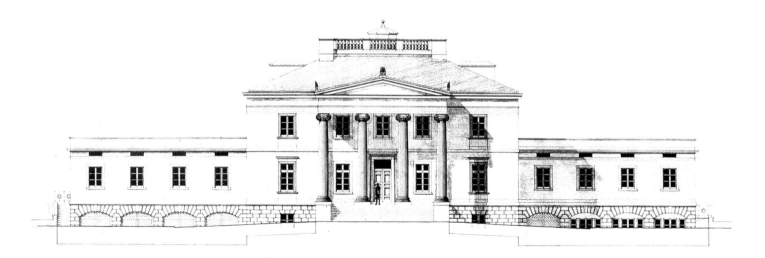

186

RIGHT
Entrance front

FACING PAGE
Drawing by Quinlan Terry of pediment at S. Maria in Campitelli, Rome (1658–74), by Carlo Rainaldi

Fawley House
Oxfordshire

In 1988 and 1989, Quinlan Terry provided an existing, dull, neo-Georgian house with a radical slap in the face in the form of a startling and sumptuous new front of flint with rich Portland stone dressings. At Fawley House, a Baroque tour de force commissioned for the Honorable David McAlpine, the rusticated Tuscan and Ionic orders break forward and backward below a bold triangular pediment containing a segmental one, inspired by Carlo

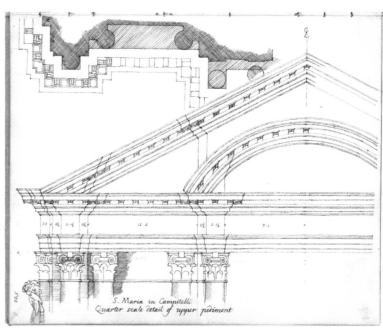

S. Maria in Campitelli
Quarter scale detail of upper pediment

Rainaldi's masterpiece, Santa Maria in Campitelli, of which Terry had made drawings in Rome. The parapet of Fawley House is crowned by seven splendid finials. The panache continues internally, where a gloomy corridor was theatrically transformed by the addition of a full-height Corinthian order, arches, and a minor Doric order, the whole effect recalling the perspective scenery by Vincenzo Scamozzi at Palladio's Teatro Olimpico (1584) at Vicenza.

191

Highland Park House

Dallas, Texas

Designed between 2000 and 2001 and built from 2002 to 2004, Highland Park House, for John and Lyn Muse, is Quinlan Terry's largest house so far, with the exception of Fort Brecqhou (see p. 164). On a palatial scale, it is nine bays long and is built on a sloping site. Thus, though the west entrance front is two stories high plus a generous attic story, the east garden, which rises from a high, rusticated basement story with a magnificent balustraded two-flight staircase leading down to the gardens on each side, is three stories plus attics. With its warm red pantiles, the high roof rises to a flat platform surrounded by a balustrade. The main nine-bay block has giant, freestanding, pedimented Ionic porticoes on both the north and south sides, but in a clever piece of orchestration, the scale is modulated downward on the east and west sides, where there are one-storied wings featuring freestanding Doric porticoes, also with pediments.

The walls at Highland Park House are of creamy yellow Texan limestone, laid on its natural bed, with dressings in cream Moleanos marble, a hard material of the "tipo Escobedas" from Spain. The whole building is tied together externally and internally by the use of the orders, following the example of Palladio—the height of the impost, columns, and entablature are the same throughout. The novel plan centers on a vast hall, nearly fifty-five feet long, considerably longer than it is wide, thus exhibiting the proportions of the grand hall, or *portega*, of Venetian palaces, particularly Baldassare Longhena's sumptuous Ca' Rezzonico (begun ca. 1667). From Terry's hall, which runs east-west through the center of the house, broad corridors lead north and south, each containing an identical staircase. The north corridor leads past the library and living room to the one-storied north wing, which contains John Muse's study, while the south corridor passes the dining room and kitchen on its way to the south wing, which contains Lyn Muse's study, a dining loggia within the south portico, and a breakfast room.

The second floor contains a family drawing room and just four large bedrooms, with bathrooms as well as numerous closets or vestibules, lobbies, and lavatories. The third floor, or attic story, provides two additional bedrooms and associated services. Facilities in the basement include a pool, media room, and an exercise room.

Balancing each other on the garden front, the two principal reception rooms—the living room and dining room (each thirty feet by twenty feet by fifteen feet high)—are provided with imposing and suitably matching articulation. This echoes the arrangement established by Terry in the interiors that he created in the house in Knightsbridge (see p. 118), where the dining room is Doric and the drawing room Corinthian, both orders linked by arches rising from high pedestals, as engraved by Palladio. At Highland Park House, the dining room is Doric, while the living room is Composite. In the living room, the monumental chimneypiece, designed by Francis Terry, features consoles and a Baroque pedimented overmantel, inspired by Longhena's pediments in his celebrated double staircase (1643–45) at the Benedictine monastery of San Giorgio Maggiore in Venice. Francis Terry's chimneypiece is surmounted by figures of the three Graces, all carved in white statuary marble.

In the dining room, with its Doric order and full triglyph frieze, the monumental chimneypiece and overmantel with a broken pediment are of Moleanos marble. The frieze is carved in the antique way with garlanded heads of the Texas longhorn, which appears on the

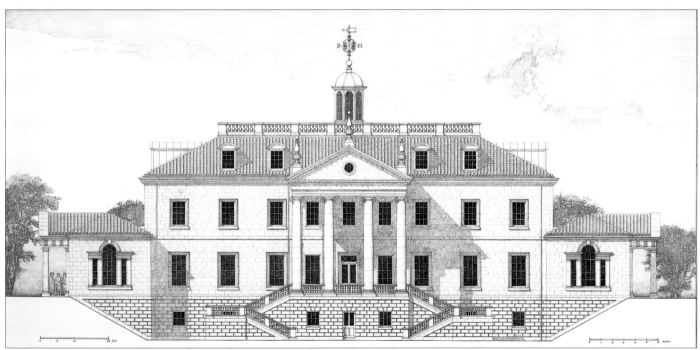

193

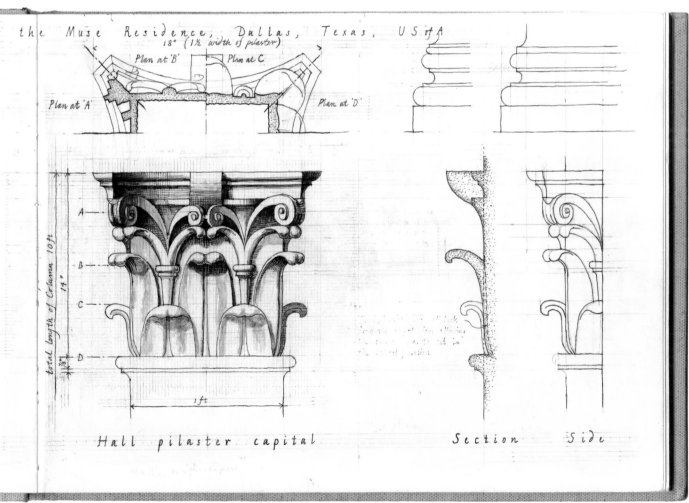

the Muse Residence, Dallas, Texas, USA

18" (1½ width of pilaster)

Plan at 'B'   Plan at C

Plan at 'A'   Plan at 'D'

total length of Column 10ft

14"

A

B

C

D

3"

1 ft

Hall pilaster capital   Section   Side

PREVIOUS PAGES
PAGE 196
Entrance hall

PAGE 197, TOP
*Entrance hall looking
east*

PAGE 197, BOTTOM
*Drawings by Francis
Terry of Corinthian
capitals in entrance
hall*

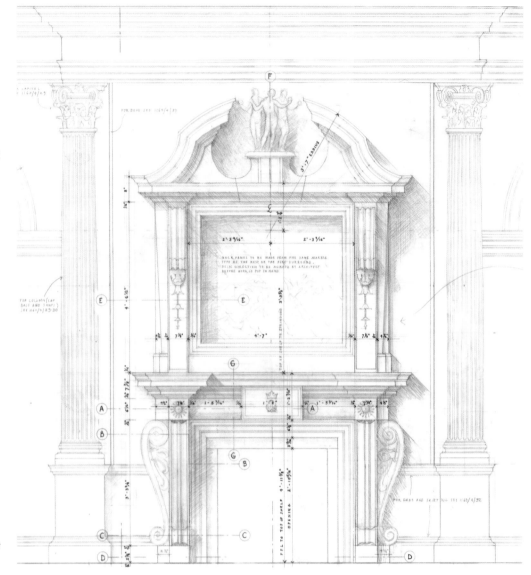

*Drawing by Francis
Terry of chimneypiece
in living room*

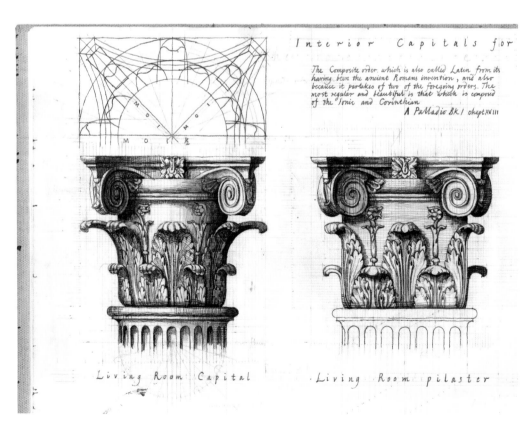

*Drawings by Francis
Terry of Composite
capitals and pilasters
in living room*

FACING PAGE
*Chimneypiece in
living room*

Chimneypiece in dining room

Detail of Doric chimneypiece in dining room, showing projecting
triglyph with swags between heads of Texas longhorns

FACING PAGE
*Drawing by Francis
Terry of Doric chim-
neypiece overmantel
in dining room*

Muse family coat of arms. Francis Terry has flanked the frieze with features that can be inter-
preted as triglyphs from a vanished Doric frieze or as consoles supporting the chimney shelf,
similar to the playful language of Raphael at the Palazzo Vidoni-Caffarelli (1515) and of
Michelangelo at the Porta Pia, both of which he measured while in Rome. Like the chimneypiece in the living room, the dining room chimneypiece was carved at Ketton in
Northamptonshire and shipped out to Texas. The interiors of this house, with high ceilings
as recommended by Palladio, and thick walls, maintain cool temperatures even when the
temperature outside is well above ninety degrees Fahrenheit, demonstrating the virtues of
solid load-bearing construction.

It is interesting to note, in conclusion, that the patron discarded a number of Ionic capitals upon arrival, a direct result of the lectures that Quinlan Terry gives in Venice on how to
draw and understand classical buildings, one of which Lyn Muse attended. When the capitals arrived on site, she could see that they lacked the refinement of the honeysuckle carving
between the echinus and the volute and that some details were also somewhat crudely
carved. The importance of having a client with sufficient understanding to be fully support-
ive of his or her architect is shown by the generous letter sent to Robert Adam in 1764 by
the Duke of Northumberland, his patron at Syon House in Middlesex. The duke wrote, "I
must desire you will order those carved mouldings which have been so ill executed by Mr.

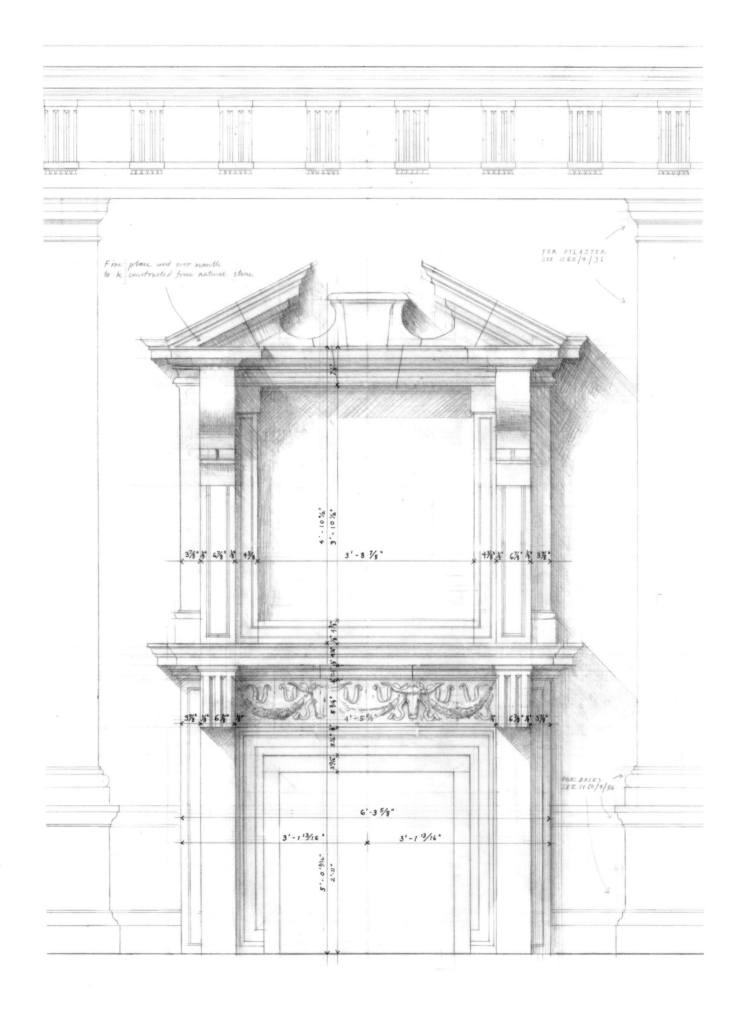

Fire place and over mantle
to be constructed from natural stone

FOR FILASTER
SEE 1160/9/36

7½"

3½" ⅛" 6⅛" ⅛" 4⅜"   3'-8 ⅞"   4⅜" ⅛" 6⅛" ⅛" 3⅜"

4'-10½"
4'-10½"

4⅜" ⅛"

8¾"   4'-5⅝"

3⅜" ⅛" 6⅞" ⅛"   ⅛" 6⅞" ⅛" 3⅜"

FOR BASES
SEE 1160/9/36

6'-3⅝"

3'-1¹³⁄₁₆"   3'-1¹³⁄₁₆"

5'-0¹⁹⁄₁₆"
2'-11"

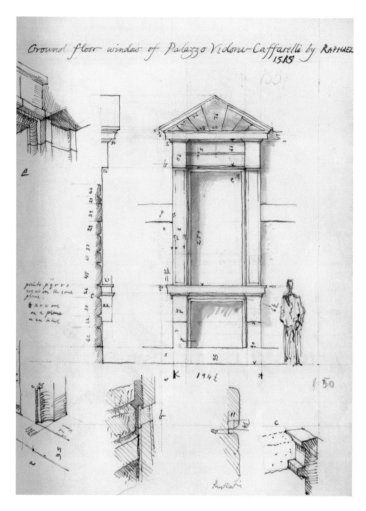

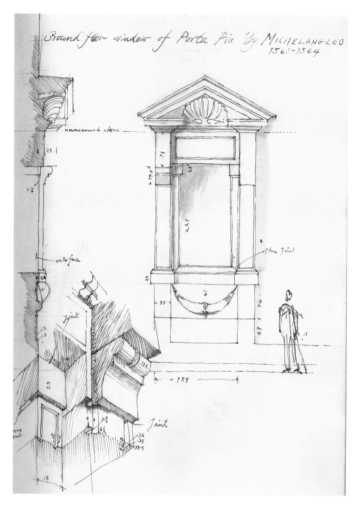

Drawing by Francis Terry of window in Palazzo Vidoni-Caffarelli, Rome (1515), attributed to Raphael

Drawing by Francis Terry of window in Porta Pia, Rome (1561–64), by Michelangelo

BELOW
Rejected capitals from main portico

FACING PAGE
South loggia

Adair to be returned to him and amended in such a manner as you shall approve of, for I would not upon any account suffer any work to be fixed up at Sion that is not completely finished to your satisfaction."

When working in Dallas at Highland Park House, Terry used a local architect, Larry Boerder, for construction. The distinguished British interior decorator, David Mlinaric, and the landscape architect, Charles Stick, also made valuable contributions.

Ferne Park

Dorset

Ferne Park is a composition of exceptional dignity, calm, and confidence, built between 2000 and 2002 for the judicious patrons Viscount and Viscountess Rothermere by an architect at the height of his powers with more than thirty years of experience behind him. It is doubtful whether any other current architect would have been capable of creating a Palladian building of this maturity and serenity in the twenty-first century. Indeed, the Georgian Group gave it the Award for the Best New Building in the Classical Tradition in 2003. It occupies a site of exceptional beauty where it replaced a large but rather featureless mid-Georgian country house, demolished before the time of the present owners. A four-square classical pile, raised on a rusticated basement story, the new Ferne Park is large in scale, yet simple, rural, and bold in character. Ornamental detail is largely confined to the north-facing entrance front, which boasts a handsome portico of four engaged columns in the Composite order.

FACING PAGE
Aerial view

Ferne Park commands views of both Dorset and Wiltshire, among the richest counties in England in building stone. Deeply rooted in the soil, and fitting harmoniously into its vast landscape, this solid, enduring construction is thus a symphony built in four stones, including the local Portland stone and the related Chilmark stone. Both are Jurassic oolitic limestones; the latter was used in Wiltshire for the building of Salisbury Cathedral in the thirteenth century, Longford Castle in the sixteenth century, and Wilton House in the seventeenth century. The principal façades at Ferne Park are of Chilmark stone, while the ornamental details, including the columns, entablature, and pediment with its giant coat of arms, the chimneys, and the rusticated basement are all done in Portland stone.

The third stone at Ferne Park, another local stone but of the post-Jurassic period, is the sandstone from the Shaftesbury district known as Upper Greensand. It has a delicate coloring of a pale, greenish gray. This was the ashlar used in eighteenth-century Dorset for major buildings such as Blandford Church (1735–39) and Sir John Vanbrugh's Eastbury (begun 1718). Ferne Park's fourth stone, the durable York stone, is used for the paving of the south terrace and front steps. Visitors approach the engaged entrance portico at Ferne Park via a broad flight of steps, equal in width to the portico and protected on each side by long cheek walls that are the same height as the basement or podium of the whole house. This disposition is derived from Roman sacred architecture, such as the Temple of Antoninus and Faustina (A.D. 141), illustrated by Palladio in his *Quattro Libri dell'Architettura*. Palladio was the medium between ancient Rome and modern England, for it was he who transferred this arrangement to domestic architecture in all four of the porticoes of his celebrated Villa Rotonda near Vicenza (1565–69).

Though the Composite order chosen for the north front of Ferne is, of course, the richest of all the classical orders, the acanthus leaves on its giant capitals, over six feet high, are plain and uncut. This follows the grand restraint of those in Palladio's largest church, San Giorgio Maggiore in Venice (1560–80). However, a novel touch was introduced in the center of the abacus of each capital between the crowning volutes where the central fleuron has attached to it a large carved bee, an emblem also in the arms of the patrons. Moreover, sculptor Andrew Tanser has carved the full coat of arms, accompanied by supporters, crest, mantling, and motto, in a cartouche in the pediment, from designs by Francis Terry. Virtually all of the houses by Palladio that he illustrated in his *Quattro Libri* feature pediments contain-

Ferne Park in the County of Dorset
for The Viscount & Viscountess Rothermere

ABOVE
Drawing by Martyn Winney
of north entrance front

FACING PAGE
North and west fronts

ing cartouches displaying the patron's arms, from which fly out carved ribbons, filling the whole pediment with lively movement. Quinlan Terry followed exactly this arrangement at Ferne Park, where the vigorous heraldic achievement is also accompanied by huge flying ribbons. A similar feature adorns the pediment of the nearby Came House (1754), a Palladian building built by John Damer to which Terry's patrons pointed as a model.

However, Terry introduced variety at Ferne by confining modillions to this pediment and to that on the south front, so they do not run emphatically around the entablature of the entire building as at Came House. This is in keeping with the view that the best architects are those who know the value of restraint. A feature of Came, and of many similar Palladian houses, is that the three windows on the top floor between the capitals of the columns are notably smaller than those in the flanking bays. The patrons of Ferne Park were anxious to avoid this crowding and imbalance, so Terry made all the upper windows of the same generous size. In the balustrade of the terrace

Temple of Antoninus and Faustina, Rome (AD 141), from Palladio, I Quattro Libri *(1570)*

on the south front, the alternate flat and pointed placing of the balusters echoes the Baroque rhythm of those at the Ca' Pesaro in Venice (1649–52), by Longhena. Current regulations in Europe forbid using balusters or banisters with spaces between them sufficiently large enough for a child's head to enter; Terry thinks that architects like Longhena, designing for the canals of Venice, may have been prompted by similar considerations.

Terry has always been reluctant to accept the mechanist ideology of twentieth-century Modernism, which assumed that current notions of function and lifestyle should dictate the entire planning and disposition of a building. By contrast, he favors a more broadly based, traditional approach, with roots in the ancient world. This produces generous, harmoniously planned spaces with unspecific functions that can thus serve a variety of changing uses. Georgian houses have thus proved infinitely more adaptable than the custom-built "functional" houses erected by architects as varied as the Gothic Revivalist Alfred Waterhouse (1830–1905) or the Modernist Le Corbusier (1887–1965).

The plan of the main floor, or piano nobile, at Ferne Park has a grand Georgian simplicity with no corridors or awkward passages. The great, rectangular, entrance hall has a stone-flagged floor and a bold screen of two unfluted Doric columns in antis carrying a triglyph frieze of imposing depth that runs all around the room. Both this room and the dining room boast new carved chimneypieces of exceptional quality. Opening off the hall to the

ABOVE LEFT
Composite capital on the north front before installation

ABOVE RIGHT
Drawing by Francis Terry of Composite capital on the north front

RIGHT
Drawing by Quinlan Terry of capital and corner of pediment at S. Giorgio Maggiore, Venice (1564–80), by Palladio

FACING PAGE
Composite capital on the north front, with heraldic bees in abacus

Detail of Ionic capital and pediment to entrance door on south front

Drawing by Quinlan Terry for balustrade on south front, echoing the Ca'Pesaro, Venice (ca. 1649–82), by Baldassare Longhena

FACING PAGE
South garden front

right is a sitting room for Lady Rothermere, well lit with windows facing west and north. Though modest in size, it has a spaciousness due to its generous height, which, like the other reception rooms on this floor, is fifteen feet. The entrance hall leads at a southwest angle to the main staircase, with its ambitious wrought-iron balustrade echoing that at Came House. The close-up view of the handsome architectural details of the large Venetian window in the middle of the west front offers those ascending the staircase further enjoyment. Terry worked with the decorator Veere Grenney in the main interiors.

Numerous outbuildings on a generous scale survive from the eighteenth-century house previously on this site. These include a vast walled kitchen garden, preceded by a stew pond, recalling the scale of a medieval monastery; a stable courtyard, to which Quinlan Terry has added a cupola; and an attractive dairy. Terry embellished and restored these exterior spaces and has also made proposals for a pool house nearby in a rustic style inspired by William Kent. His design harmonizes stylistically with the cascade, which has been restored by Lady Rothermere. Terry worked with the landscape architect Rupert Golby to further enhance the setting of the new house.

LEFT
*Entrance hall, looking east
from the staircase*

BELOW
*Entrance hall, showing
chimneypiece and Doric
screen*

Cambridge

Downing College

HOWARD BUILDING

The Fellows of Downing College voted for the approval of Quinlan Terry's Howard Building (1986–89) in 1983, not so much because he promised classical forms, but because they were persuaded that any building by him would be solidly constructed and would have a long life. Cambridge was by now acutely aware of the structural and environmental failures that afflict high-tech Modernist glass buildings—James Stirling's famous History Faculty Building (1964–67), for example, was visibly decaying and surrounded by a wire fence labeled "Dangerous Structure. Keep Out." Members of the History Faculty came within one vote of demolishing it and replacing it with something more sensible.

A precursor to Terry's Howard Building at Downing College in Cambridge was the elaborate summer house he built between 1980 and 1982 for Michael (now Lord) Heseltine at Thenford in Northamptonshire. Terry explains that in this exceptionally rich design with

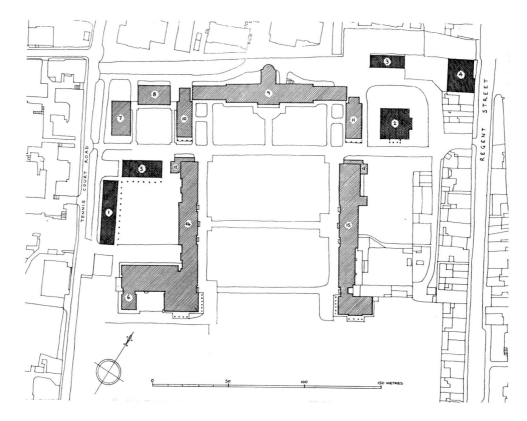

1. RESIDENTIAL BUILDING	QUINLAN TERRY	1995
2. MAITLAND ROBINSON LIBRARY	QUINLAN TERRY	1994
3. JCR	QUINLAN TERRY	1991
4. RICHMOND HOUSE	QUINLAN TERRY	1991
5. HOWARD BUILDING	QUINLAN TERRY	1987
6. SCR	W. HOWELL	1969
7. KENNY B	A. SCOTT	1953-62
8. KENNY A	A. SCOTT	1953-62
9. NORTH RANGE	BAKER AND SCOTT	
10. WEST WING TO NORTH RANGE	H. BAKER	1910-31
11. EAST WING TO NORTH RANGE	H. BAKER	1910-31
12. ADDITION TO WEST RANGE	E M BARRY	1873
13. ADDITION TO EAST RANGE	E M BARRY	1873
14. WEST RANGE	W. WILKINS	1809-20
15. EAST RANGE	W. WILKINS	1809-20

a strong Baroque flavor "the use of numbers governs the design, with the intercolumniation being three at the ends, four at the sides, and five in the middle. All proportions relate to the bottom diameter in whole imperial numbers." This mathematical balance is combined with a pictorial quality provided by the polychromatic contrast between the golden brown Hornton stone used for the walling and the creamy white Clipsham stone used for the orders, Corinthian alternating with Composite, which he first noticed while measuring Bramante's two-storied colonnade in his cloister at Santa Maria della Pace in Rome (1500).

Similarly, the Howard Building at Downing College has walls of pale brown Ketton stone contrasting with Portland stone for pedestals, columns, pilasters, entablature, door surrounds, and finials. Its lavish materials are matched by rich ornament and rustication, as well as a mannerist game played with false windows. In this complex and clever building, Terry set himself the challenging task of incorporating all four orders. Since it is dedicated to the theater and the performing arts, the columns marking the main entrance on the north front are in the festive Composite and Corinthian orders. This contrasts with the severe neoclassicism of the earliest buildings at Downing from 1807 to 1820 by William Wilkins, though even he tempered his Grecian austerity in his unexecuted designs for the chapel with the Roman Corinthian order. On the entrance front and two short sides of the Howard Building, the Corinthian pilasters and engaged Composite columns are carried on a high plinth, but this

TOP
*Howard Building, south front, from the Doric
colonnade of residential building in Howard Court*

ABOVE
*Drawing by Quinlan Terry of Piazza della Madonna,
Loreto, Italy*

RIGHT
*Residential building, east front built in 1994
with Howard Building colonnade to the right*

disappears on the south front where, instead, there is a one-storied projecting colonnade or loggia of baseless Roman Doric columns, surmounted by a lively balustrade inspired by that in the Piazza della Madonna at Loreto, drawn by Terry in 1982. Lastly, the Ionic order is represented in the Howard Building by the pilasters in the second-floor auditorium.

Even though Terry was himself a member of the Royal Fine Art Commission from 1996 to 1998, a pamphlet of advice published by that body condemned the Howard Building on three separate occasions, saying "even if not an actual copy, [the Howard Building] is a repetition of what has been," while its "classical decoration is not much more than a veneer." Instead, buildings held up for imitation were a new power station at Bexley; the Economist group of buildings, a concrete pile by Peter and Alison Smithson that violates the profile of Saint James's Street; and Michael Hopkins's Financial Times building, which is pretentiously described as embodying "the principle of showing how the building is put together by articulating the structure [that] supports the glass wall."

Criticism of the Howard Building came from the distinguished architectural critic Gavin Stamp in the *Architects' Journal* in March 1988, even though he had previously written in praise of Terry's work in *Architectural Digest*. His condemnation of the handling of the classical language in the Howard Building and of its "sham" features were refuted, respectively, in two accompanying essays by the distinguished architectural historian Sir John Summerson, and by the architect Léon Krier. Summerson explained, "I had an opposite opinion to Stamp where the exterior is concerned. My own first view of the building gave me a rare shock of pleasure. Here was a façade with something new to say in a language that I happen to understand and love. The general proportions and the distribution of openings seemed absolutely right: the Corinthian order took my fancy—it has been carefully studied." Krier claimed that "if applied universally, Stamp's criticisms would indeed have to condemn the majority of Classical buildings in Cambridge and the world. It is that kind of moralistic radicalism that established and maintains Modernism's intolerant reign." Stamp's article, and the essays by Summerson and Krier, were reprinted for an American audience in the journal *Progressive Architecture*, in July 1988.

Osberton Park, Nottinghamshire, ca. 1805, by William Wilkins, from George Richardson, New Vitruvius Britannicus, *vol II, 1808*

FACING PAGE
Maitland Robinson Library, entrance portico on south front

FOLLOWING PAGES
Maitland Robinson Library, from the southeast, with range of 1930–32 by Sir Herbert Baker on the left

Carving of the snake-entwined staff of Aesculapius, god of medicine, in the frieze of the Maitland Robinson Library

FACING PAGE, TOP LEFT
Drawing by Francis Terry of console from doorway in the Medici Chapel, S. Lorenzo, Florence (1520–34), by Michelangelo

FACING PAGE, TOP RIGHT
Entrance doorway, Maitland Robinson Library

FACING PAGE, BOTTOM LEFT
Plasterwork designed by Francis Terry, Maitland Robinson Library staircase hall, incorporating the griffin in the coat of arms of Downing College

FACING PAGE, BOTTOM RIGHT
Working drawing by Francis Terry for plasterwork in the Maitland Robinson Library staircase hall

HOWARD COURT

Terry's Howard Court at Downing College, a three-storied range of chambers eleven bays long, continues the Doric colonnade of the Howard Building (see p. 224) at right angles to it but as an open internal passageway. Casement windows on the top story echo those in the nearby buildings from 1930 to 1932 and 1950 to 1953 by Sir Herbert Baker and A. T. Scott. A generous building of Ketton stone with widely spaced windows below broadly projecting Tuscan eaves—a development of Terry's houses in Frog Meadow in Dedham—Howard Court is popular with the undergraduates who live in it.

MAITLAND ROBINSON LIBRARY

Terry built the square-planned Maitland Robinson Library (1990–92) at Downing College of load-bearing Ketton stone. Its many Grecian references remind one of Wilkins's scholarly knowledge of Athenian architecture, and include a powerful Greek Doric portico inspired by the gateway into the Roman Agora (10 B.C.) in Athens, and Wilkins's own unexecuted Greek Doric porter's lodge for Downing College, inspired by the Propylaea in Athens (439–432 B.C.). Additionally, the portico of Terry's library, especially in its relation to the rest of the building, echoes Wilkins's now-demolished portico of about 1805 at Osberton Park in Nottinghamshire. The metopes in the Doric frieze of the library are filled with large-scale carved symbols representing the subjects taught and studied in the college. The doorcase in the portico combines Greek work, including canted architraves, with references to Michelangelo's elegant doorcases in his Medici chapel in Florence (begun 1520). The capriccio of Athenian references includes the octagonal tower surmounting the library, inspired by the Tower of the Winds in Athens (1st century B.C.), and the eastern portico, which is indebted to the now-destroyed Choragic Monument of Thrasyllus (319 B.C.) on the Acropolis. The top-lit octagonal staircase hall contains panels of stucco decoration designed by Francis Terry and inspired by those of the Ara Pacis in Rome.

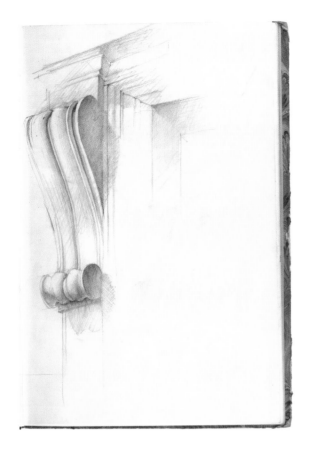

*Richmond House,
Regent Street,
1989–90*

RICHMOND HOUSE

Terry also provided Downing College with a modest, one-storied, freestanding Junior Combination Room that resembles a garden pavilion, as well as Richmond House, a range of shops and offices that fits effortlessly into Regent Street, next to the college. Terry's work

is recorded in a handsome volume of scholarship, *Committed to Classicism: The Building of Downing College, Cambridge* (1987), by Cinzia Maria Sicca, an architectural historian and Fellow of Downing College.

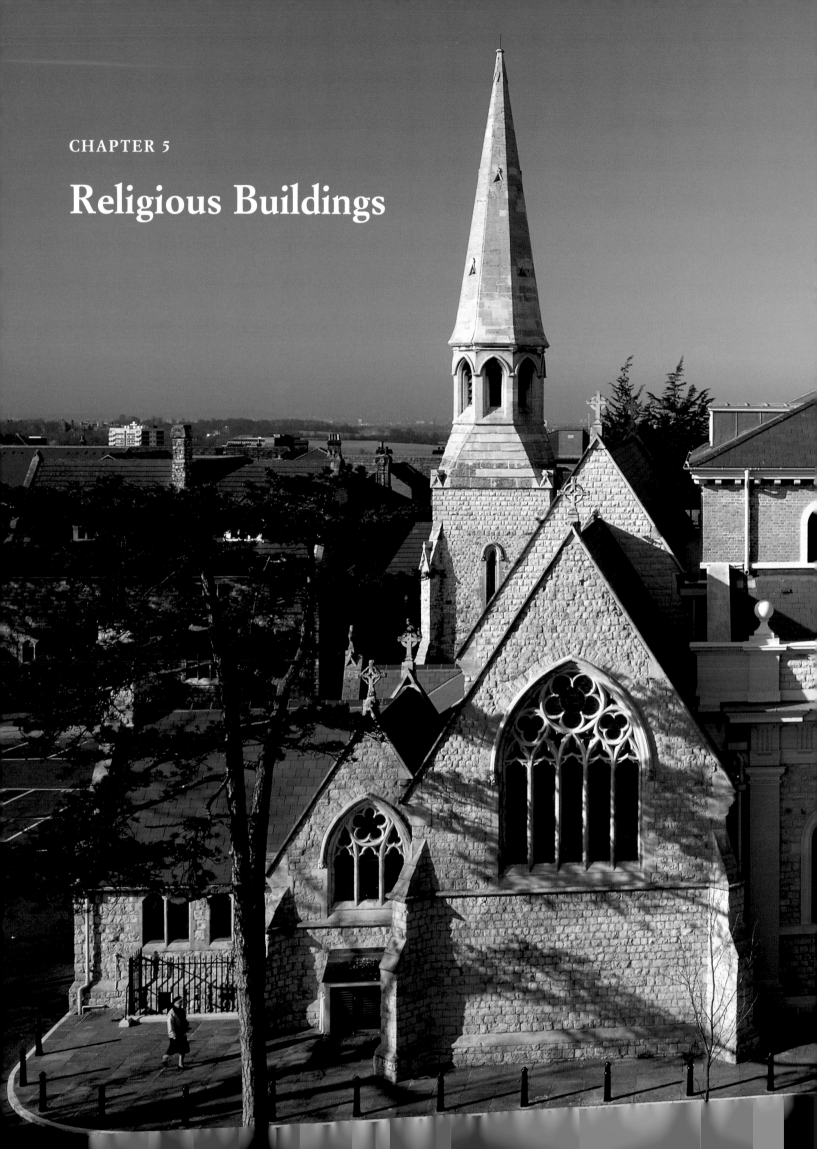

CHAPTER 5

Religious Buildings

House of Worship
Tehran

PREVIOUS PAGES
Brentwood Cathedral, Essex, 1989–91, with Victorian church to the left

BELOW
Plans, section, and elevations of first design. Drawing by Quinlan Terry, exhibited at the Royal Academy Summer Exhibition, 1975

FACING PAGE
Drawing by Quinlan Terry of west window, Dedham Church, Essex, ca. 1500

Quinlan Terry's first design for a major religious building was the House of Worship, or temple, for the Baha'i religion on a mountainous site near Tehran in Iran. From 1972, before Raymond Erith's death, to 1977, Terry made designs for this great domed building with elements drawn from many classical buildings in Italy, notably Venice, as well as buildings in Spain, the Middle East, and even England (visible in the Gothic windows he inserted over the main entrance, inspired by one in Dedham Church). The clients of the Tehran House of Worship felt the mingling of classical and Gothic details of the design paralleled their beliefs. Though never executed because of the revolution in Persia, Terry's building was, significantly, centrally planned, like his two major completed churches, for the Roman Catholic Church and the Anglican Church.

236

2.4 > 6 < 2.4 > 12

Dedham Church. West Window

½" Scale.   4th Nov 93

Brentwood Cathedral

Essex

The Roman Catholic Cathedral of Saint Mary and Saint Helen at Brentwood in Essex, built between 1989 and 1991, demonstrates clearly the complexities at the heart of Quinlan Terry's work because, though this building is dependent on the language of architects such as Brunelleschi, Bramante, and Wren, it looks like no other Catholic cathedral. By contrast, the building that it largely replaced looked depressingly like a thousand other churches: it was a coarse ragstone Gothic building of 1861, further disfigured in the 1970s by a mean, Modernist extension in reinforced concrete, which resembled the entrance to a post office or clinic. It had structural problems and was demolished to make way for Terry's work. The new cathedral is radical in that, though in function it responds to the liturgical reforms of the Second Vatican Council, it uniquely demonstrates that those changes can be accommodated in architecturally traditional forms, as opposed to the Modernist language that had been universally adopted after the Council.

To demolish almost an entire cathedral was, of course, a very emotive matter and aroused complaints from some members of the congregation and residents of the town of Brentwood. The bishop of Brentwood, the Right Reverend Thomas McMahon, was therefore obliged to take the matter to a planning appeal in order to obtain planning permission. Once again, Terry's radical classicism met with opposition, and once again he was to work in close harmony with an articulate patron, the bishop of Brentwood, one of the few Catholic bishops in England with any aesthetic sensibility.

The external walls of Brentwood Cathedral are of ragstone, with the classical elements in smooth Portland stone. Set back behind a balustrade is a clerestory of Smead Dean yellow stock brick with a pyramidal roof of Welsh slate and a domed octagonal lantern. The beautiful entrance portico, with its ring of freestanding Doric columns, is inspired by Wren's porticoes on the transepts of Saint Paul's Cathedral and Gibbs's at Saint Mary-le-Strand. These were themselves dependent on Pietro da Cortona's entrance to the church of Santa Maria della Pace in Rome (1656–59), which was indebted to the circular temples of the ancient world. The Doric order of Terry's portico, with a full triglyph and metope frieze, is carried around the first-floor exterior, and appears at the same level around the centrally planned interior, above a Tuscan arcade that recalls that of Brunelleschi's Ospedale degli Innocenti in Florence (1419–44).

The internal disposition is organized around an utterly novel axis that runs not east-west but instead north-south from the entrance portico, past an *ambo*, or lectern, to a centrally placed altar, with the bishop's throne beyond. Seating is disposed on all three sides of the altar. Remarkably, Terry has utilized this unique plan for a variety of religious buildings. In 1993, when he was invited to redesign the interior of the medieval church of Saint Helen's in Bishopsgate (see p. 248) for an Anglican evangelical parish, he produced a very similar plan, as he did in 1996 in the remodeling of the Victorian Gothic Christ Church at Bromley in Kent. There, he transferred the axis from the communion table at the east end to a new pulpit and lectern in the center of the north side of the nave, arranging seating around it on three sides.

The east-west axis at Brentwood terminates at each end in a Venetian window in the Ionic order, while the sumptuous organ case and bishop's throne are in the Corinthian and Composite orders. Thus, all five orders feature in a building that is put together with such

PREVIOUS PAGES
PAGE 238
House of Worship, Tehran. Typical porch. Drawing by Quinlan Terry, exhibited at the Royal Academy Summer Exhibition, 1977

PAGE 239
House of Worship, Tehran. South elevation. Drawing by Quinlan Terry exhibited at the Royal Academy Summer Exhibition, 1977

FACING PAGE
Brentwood Cathedral, Essex, 1989–91 p. 241 Drawing by Les Edwards, exhibited at the oyal AcademySummer Exhibition, 1992

FOLLOWING PAGES
North entrance front

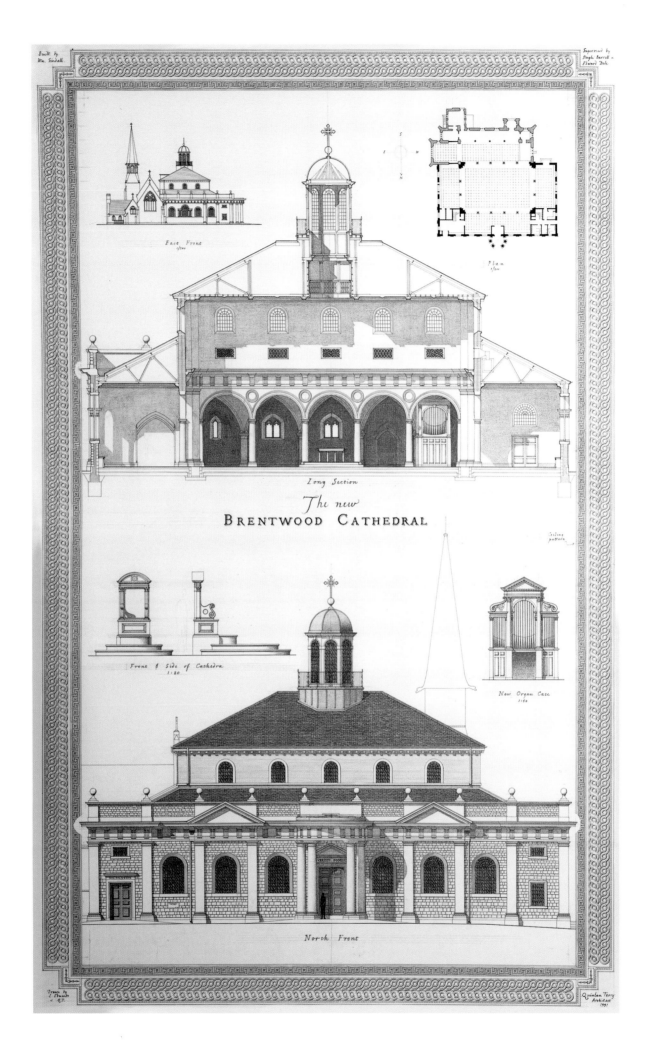

Built by
Wm. Sindall

Supervised by
Hugh Barrett
Flavel Dale

East Front
1/200

Plan
1/200

Long Section

The new
BRENTWOOD CATHEDRAL

Front & Side of Cathedra
1/20

New Organ Case
1/50

North Front

Drawn by
L. Edwards
& Q.T.

Quinlan Terry
Architect
1987

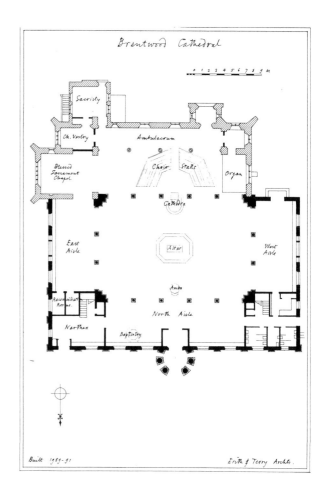

beautiful logic that exterior is united with interior in a visually and functionally satisfying way. In the spandrels of the arcade are the Stations of the Cross in the form of terra-cotta roundels carved by sculptor Raphael Maklouf (b. 1937), inspired in their placing by Andrea della Robbia's plaques at the Ospedale in Florence. In the design of the bishop's throne, Terry was influenced by that at San Miniato al Monte in Florence, a church that was begun in 1062 as the most elegant example of the "Tuscan proto-Renaissance." A monumental object of Nabresina marble that will last for a thousand years and more, the throne at Brentwood reflects in its durable and rare materials the dignity and merit of the office of the bishop. It is worthy of much contemplation for it is an object lesson in how knowledge of the orders can enhance and contribute to the design of furniture, as much as of a building. It is approached up two steps in the form of platforms with semicircular terminations. The handling of space and mass on four levels is logical and satisfying, functional and beautiful.

The bishop of Brentwood also enabled Terry to create a new urban scene into which the cathedral fits. The cathedral forms the south side of a courtyard that Terry has sympathetically embellished, providing new railings, adapting a Victorian chapel as a song school, and adding a presbytery, parish hall, and new office entrance in the form of a three-bay, two-storied, pedimented façade, with a Doric order on the first floor and Ionic on the second. This neatly fits between existing Victorian Gothic and modern office buildings. In a recent local survey the cathedral was chosen as "Brentwood's best loved building." The startling juxtaposition at Brentwood Cathedral of Terry's work with the surviving aisle and spire of the previous Victorian Gothic building recalls the ancient colleges of Oxford and Cambridge, where at King's College for example, the Palladian Baroque Gibbs building confronts the Perpendicular Gothic chapel.

Saint Helen's

Bishopsgate, London

From 1993 to 1995, Quinlan Terry carried out a major remodeling of an ancient and complex building, the church of Saint Helen at Bishopsgate, in the city of London. This historic church includes the remains of the nuns' church from a partly demolished thirteenth-century Benedictine nunnery, which itself incorporated an earlier parish church. Thus, the church has, oddly, what seem to be two parallel naves. Miraculously, it survived the Great Fire of London in 1666 as well as bomb damage in the World War II, so the changes proposed by the parish in 1993, with Terry as architect, were understandably the subject of debate. However, alterations and enrichments in both the pre-Reformation and post-Reformation periods had been made in every century from the fourteenth to the twentieth. As a result of the explosion of IRA bombs near the church in April 1992 and again in April 1993, the roof had been raised and had not returned to its true position, windows were blown out, destroying their stonework, and monuments were seriously damaged. Thus, no one could doubt in 1993 that extensive repair work was necessary.

In a reordering that took place between 1892 and 1893 by the major Gothic Revival architect John Loughborough Pearson, screens and stalls were provided in the south transept to reflect the liturgical pattern of High Church worship that then prevailed. However, between the 1960s and 1990s, a contrasting tradition of Anglican Evangelical worship was established, which led to the church becoming a hugely popular center of biblical preaching that focused on the pulpit rather than on the altar or holy table. The IRA bomb damage provided an opportunity for the parish to remodel the interior yet again to suit the new liturgical use.

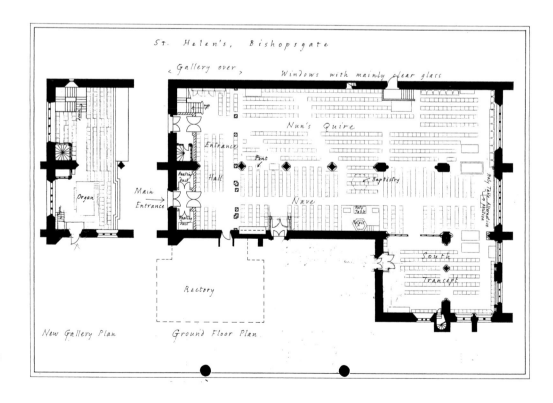

RIGHT
Plan

FACING PAGE
Medieval west entrance front with cupola of ca.1700

If historic buildings are to live, there is no reason why they should not continue to be adapted as they have been in the past, as long as the changes are made with taste and skill on the basis of historical knowledge. One would certainly not consider unleashing on a beautiful and historic church such as Saint Helen's the typical Modernist architect who, inevitably, lacks the skills, knowledge, or even inclination, to use traditional forms. Terry's proposals, made at the request of the parish authorities, involved removing and resiting Pearson's chancel screens; raising the floor, which Pearson had lowered, by three feet; adding a gallery at the west end; opening up a new, stone-framed, entrance doorway; constructing new roofs; resiting monuments; and taking out the Victorian pews.

It was Terry's aim to diminish the Victorian, High Church flavor of the building by returning it to its circa-1800 character as a Georgian preaching box. Thus, the church today, as reordered by Terry, has a different character from that which it had from 1892 to 1992. It is in fact a strikingly beautiful interior with more visual coherence than it has had since the sixteenth century. At a meeting held in the church in November 1992, Terry explained his

Eighteenth-century engraving of the interior, showing a gallery at the west end and a level floor

proposals to representatives from English Heritage, the Society for the Protection of Ancient Buildings, the Ancient Monuments Society, the Victorian Society, the Friends of Friendless Churches, the Georgian Group, and the Council for the Care of Places of Worship. It was a daunting occasion because the representatives of all of these institutions, except the last two, opposed the proposals. As a result, the English Heritage inspector, Harry Duckett, remarked, "This has all the making of a cause célèbre."

The objections to Quinlan Terry's plans for restoration and reordering, presented by the rector and churchwardens, were considered by the Consistory Court of the Diocese of London at a hearing with the chancellor as judge, occupying some nine days between June 15 and July 26, 1993. The queen's counsel representing the parish, known as the petitioners, called seven witnesses; the counsel for English Heritage called three; the Corporation of London and the Society for the Protection of Ancient Buildings, one each; the Victorian Society, two; while the judge's five witnesses represented the Council for the Care of Churches, the London Diocesan Advisory Committee, and the Museum of London. The judge's report of the hearing, which found in favor of Terry's proposals, is a document of eighty-four pages. The text of Terry's proof of evidence is itself forty-six pages. It was a monumental and costly trial, unique in English architectural and ecclesiastical history, which involved the evidence and the time of numerous distinguished clergymen, architects, and academics.

The judge cited a celebrated passage from the judgment of Lord Penzance in the Arches Court of Canterbury in 1892, which also concerned proposals to alter a church. Lord Penzance argued that "the appellants have put forward their attachment to the old church and its interesting connection with times gone by; but they seem to forget that the sacred edifice has a future as well as a past. It belongs not to any one generation." The judge in 1993 thus reminded the court that matters of conservation had played a part in church planning long before twentieth-century Ancient Monuments and Town and Country Planning legislation. In the end, inspector Duckett's prophecy that the opposition to Terry's designs at Saint Helen's had "the making of a cause célèbre" did not come true. The work was carried out and has not caused any further controversy, though it was predictably criticized in Nikolaus Pevsner's book *The City of London* (1997), part of the Buildings of England series, on the astonishing grounds that Terry had shown "no sense of a creative dialogue between past and present."

Since much of the opposition to Terry's proposals centered on raising the level of the church's floor, he carried out an enormously thorough historical survey of the building with the help of contemporary drawings in the archives of the Leathersellers' Company. As a result of this process, he was able to show that the floor of the two naves had been uniform in 1808, at a level three feet higher than at present. Returning the floor to this level would make access easier for the vast numbers who use the church and would suit its new role as an assembly hall for preaching. It would also be an aesthetic improvement, for the new floor

Nineteenth-century engraving of the interior, showing a level floor at the east end

would be at the correct height in relation to the bases of the fifteenth-century columns of the nave arcade, which Pearson, when he lowered the floor in the 1890s, had left stranded in midair. His reason for lowering the floor had been largely liturgical, because it allowed steps to be constructed up to the altar in conformity with High Church practice. Ironically, the Society for the Protection of Ancient Buildings, which objected so strongly to Terry's proposals, had been violently opposed to Pearson's work in the 1890s!

In raising the floor in the south transept to the same level as that in the nave, Terry was putting it back to its position in the eighteenth century, though it had been lower in the Middle Ages. Restoring the floor to its eighteenth-century level created a void underneath, in which heating and sound reinforcement systems could be accommodated. It also provided sufficient depth for a hexagonal baptistery to be built into the floor in front of the pulpit. This is normally unobtrusively covered by wooden boards.

Referring in his proof of evidence at the Consistory Court to his "attempt to give a historical account of the building," Terry explained, "I hasten to say that I am not an architectural historian . . . my primary interest is not history but *architecture*; the elements of which are (to quote Sir Henry Wotton) 'Firmness, Commodity and Delight.'. . . History is not the first ingredient of architecture. There has been much criticism of the proposals from the narrow perspective of history. It is significant that there has been no criticism or reservations expressed on aesthetics; on the way these proposals achieve a consistent and attractive building." Nor, he might have added, on the remarkable fact that he had been able to double the seating capacity of the church from five hundred to one thousand.

In December 1995, Terry gave a lecture at the church, repeated to the Georgian Group in 1997, in which he explained the principles he used in adding to a historic building, but which the "philosophy" of English Heritage had opposed at every turn. Agreeing with the judgment of Lord Penzance on those who had forgotten that "the sacred edifice has a future as well as a past," he recalled how "the objectors saw the church nostalgically as a mass of masonry and woodwork to be preserved, mummified, and embalmed. Behind all the objections raised to our proposals there was a strong undercurrent of disapproval with our

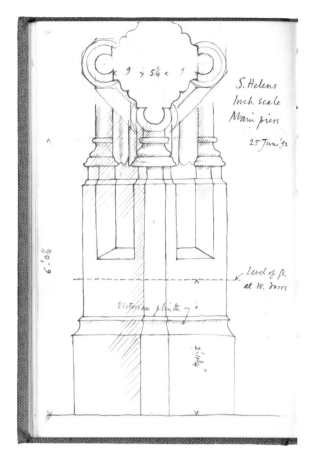

ABOVE LEFT
Drawing by Quinlan Terry of the existing piers, showing the level of the original floor and the additional pedestal inserted by J. L. Pearson

ABOVE RIGHT
New east window

emphasis on a preaching ministry, so characteristic of Wren's city churches. We were constantly lampooned in the press and [the popular satirical magazine] *Private Eye*; on one occasion someone asked, 'why can't these Essex men worship in a concrete garage in Dagenham?'" In less insensitive language, the astonishing recommendation that the parish should move out of its own church was actually made by an English Heritage inspector.

Terry went on to confess, "What I have had to contend with, in the main, are not facts but the *opinions* of art historians who have a particular view . . . [which] put simply, is that anything that is old, whether good or bad, must not be disturbed because it is old; it is as if history has stopped (probably about five years ago), and from now onwards architects must use their skill to preserve every piece of existing fabric, regardless of its use"—and, English Heritage would add, of its quality.

The complaint, in Pevsner's *City of London*, that Terry had not engaged in "creative dialogue" with the church, is disproved by many features of his work here, notably by the dignified timber gallery resting on Doric columns with a triglyph frieze that he ran across the whole west end. Based on hints of what had existed earlier as shown in an engraving, this appropriate addition to the church must be the first of its kind to be built for nearly two centuries, yet it looks as though it has been there forever. The best place from which to view the whole church, it is also technically an improvement on its Georgian predecessors, since the stepped seating for one hundred worshippers that it provides is generous and comfortably disposed. The gallery is approached by a handsome new staircase, which, with its turned balusters, is of the decent, unpretentious form characterized by Terry as "the Gray's Inn type."

Another advantage of the new gallery is that it has made possible the return to this part of the church of the fine 1742 organ, which had been unaccountably moved into an obscure

250

position in the south transept. Terry has also incorporated Pearson's parclose choir screens into the first floor of the gallery, where they serve effortlessly as wall paneling in this new sheltered space that welcomes the visitor on arrival and provides an attractive frame for views eastward.

There was much debate as to the replacement for the great east window of the nun's choir, or northern nave, following its destruction as a result of bomb damage. The old window had been of five lights, which Terry believed were disagreeably broad in relation to the overall proportion of the window. He found a more satisfactory pattern in a fifteenth-century window of six lights from the church of Saint-Sauveur at Dinan in Brittany; it contains Flamboyant tracery, not dissimilar to English Decorated but more vigorous. This he adapted for Saint Helen's, where the finished product, with its broad mullions and flowing forms, provides an unexpected but appropriate addition to the church.

In the west wall of the south transept Terry provided a new door, for an additional exit was required by the fire officer and was also considered desirable by the parish, enabling latecomers to arrive at services unobtrusively. A Modernist architect would have chosen a "frankly modern" design in steel and glass; a more timid one would have chosen something bland and neutral in light varnished oak. Terry chose neither, but once again entered into a "creative dialogue" with the church. The easiest solution would have been a modest Gothic doorway, which might be considered appropriate to a medieval church. Instead, he adopted a bolder solution, yet one drawing on the previous history of the building: He partly replaced the remains of one of the modest, thirteenth-century lancets in the rubble wall of the transept with a handsome new classical doorway. With its emphatic form and eared surround, he boldly contributed to the mannerist language of the doorways that were added to the church in the seventeenth century.

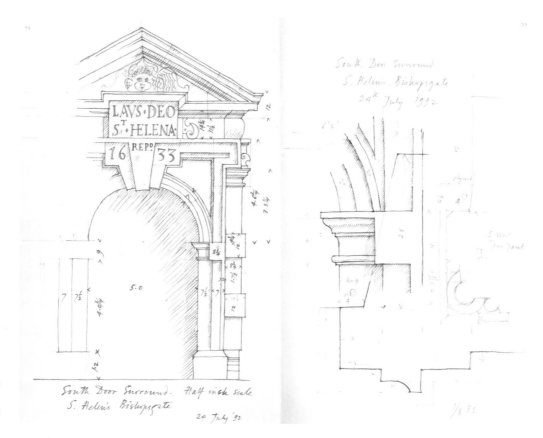

Terry's doorway recalls the two sophisticated doorways by Sanmicheli at his Porta Palio at Verona of the 1550s. A tablet over the door, occupied at the Porta Palio by a swagged heraldic cartouche, is here carved with the inscription in Trajan lettering, "Heaven and earth will pass away but my words will never pass away." The crisp and succulent moldings of the series of lavish carved frames to Terry's doorway emphasise the pleasure that the Christian

can legitimately take in the things of this world, whilst realising that, as the inscription makes clear, they are essentially temporal. This doorway alone would justify our description of his architecture as "radical." Not surprisingly, Terry has said of this commission that it has given him more satisfaction than any other. It is also expected that from 2006 English Heritage is to adopt a more understanding and sympathetic approach to stylistically sensitive and appropriate adaptations of historic buildings.

A building such as St Helen's has a future as well as a past; it also has a present. This understanding of the relevance of the past to the buildings of today and their continuation tomorrow has, in our present throw-away society, meant that Terry has had to swim against the tide all his life. Whether his work will help turn the tide to the extent that major public buildings will once again embody traditional values, and that he and his companions will thereby become establishment, rather than radical, figures, is not the primary subject of this book. Only time will tell.

INDEX

Note: Page numbers in *italic* indicate photographs and drawings.

PHOTOGRAPHY CREDITS